# Mindfulness

Start Sleeping Better, Release Stress and Overcome Depression and Anxiety

(A Practical Guide for Changing Thoughts, Beliefs, and Emotional Reactions)

**Daniel Linton**

Published by Rob Miles

© **Daniel Linton**

All Rights Reserved

*Mindfulness: Start Sleeping Better, Release Stress and Overcome Depression and Anxiety (A Practical Guide for Changing Thoughts, Beliefs, and Emotional Reactions)*

ISBN 978-1-989990-80-3

All rights reserved. No part of this guide may be reproduced in any form without permission in writing from the publisher except in the case of brief quotations embodied in critical articles or reviews.

Legal & Disclaimer

The information contained in this book is not designed to replace or take the place of any form of medicine or professional medical advice. The information in this book has been provided for educational and entertainment purposes only.

The information contained in this book has been compiled from sources deemed reliable, and it is accurate to the best of the Author's knowledge; however, the Author cannot guarantee its accuracy and validity and cannot be held liable for any errors or omissions. Changes are periodically made to this book. You must consult your doctor or get professional medical advice before using any of the suggested remedies, techniques, or information in this book.

Upon using the information contained in this book, you agree to hold harmless the Author from and against any damages, costs, and expenses, including any legal fees potentially resulting from the application of any of the information provided by this guide. This disclaimer applies to any damages or injury caused by the use and application, whether directly or indirectly, of any advice or information presented, whether for breach of contract, tort, negligence, personal injury, criminal intent, or under any other cause of action.

You agree to accept all risks of using the information presented inside this book. You need to consult a professional medical practitioner in order to ensure you are both able and healthy enough to participate in this program.

# Table of Contents

INTRODUCTION .................................................................... 1

CHAPTER 1: WHAT IS TYPE A BEHAVIOR? .......................... 6

CHAPTER 2: HISTORY OF MINDFULNESS .......................... 14

CHAPTER 3: THE BENEFITS OF MINDFULNESS MEDITATION ............................................................................ 18

CHAPTER 4: 21 DAYS OF MINDFULNESS .......................... 29

CHAPTER 5: THE NEED TO KNOW ................................... 50

CHAPTER 6: FINDING YOUR FOCUS .................................. 55

CHAPTER 7: MEDITATION TECHNIQUES FOR BEGINNERS 62

CHAPTER 8: WHAT ARE NEGATIVE EMOTIONS? .............. 75

CHAPTER 9: MINDFULNESS DURING YOUR COMMUTE .... 92

CHAPTER 10: USING MINDFULNESS TO OVERCOME ANXIETY ..................................................................... 107

CHAPTER 11: INSTILL COMPASSION IN YOUR CHILD ...... 114

CHAPTER 12: HUMAN BEING VS. HUMAN DOING ......... 122

CHAPTER 13: ENGAGING THE SENSES ........................... 137

CHAPTER 14: THE PRACTICE OF MINDFULNESS MEDITATION .................................................................. 142

CHAPTER 15: ENJOY SPIRITUAL AWARENESS ................. 151

CHAPTER 16: STEP BY STEP INSTRUCTIONS ON HOW TO PERFORM MEDITATION: .............................................. 157

CHAPTER 17: TAKE FIVE MINUTES .................................. 166

CHAPTER 18: MINDFUL MEDITATION FOR FAMILY STRESS .................................................................................. 172

CHAPTER 19: WHY YOU SHOULD VISUALIZE .................. 184

CONCLUSION ................................................................. 189

**Introduction**

This book explores all the ways you can use meditation to build concentration, supercharge your focus and become mindful in everyday life. If you follow along and do the exercises you will begin to see changes to your everyday experience that build exponentially.

Before we begin, let's talk a little bit about the word "mindfulness." Unfortunately, most of the information and techniques you may have read about "mindfulness" are watered down versions of the real stuff. The aim of this series is to present the art of concentration (and insight in later volumes) as a practical, pragmatic meditation system. You may even find yourself getting more creative, feeling more relaxed and happier in general. While those are usually the selling points of a mindfulness practice, here here they will be treated as pleasant side-effects to the real work.

We will start your practice on the cushion but eventually the goal is to quickly get you practicing out in real life so you can spend most of your waking hours mindfully aware.

I've spent years studying, practicing and learning from books, online instruction and even real-live monks, the often simple secrets of mindfulness. A lot of the information isn't so much shrouded in secrecy as it is clouded by dogma, belief systems and ritual. We will avoid all of that superfluous information unless I feel it adds to the practice. These are the real-deal hardcore techniques used by many people on the path. I've done all the legwork and will only present techniques that have worked for me and others consistently and reliably.

During the course of the book, I keep jargon and special words to a minimum.

We're going to keep this conversational. There are just a few rules that I ask you to follow as best you can while reading the book. Once you've finished the book and have some competency with the techniques, you should begin to explore. But these general guidelines will help you stay on track in the beginning and get the most benefits as quickly as possible.

Follow instructions precisely at first. There is plenty of time to explore and riff on the techniques later. But for now, it's important that you learn and become proficient with the basics.

Practice every day. I'm providing you with a very specific and powerful recipe for developing your concentration and expanding your mind. To get the greatest benefit from this practice you need to build-up momentum and get the dose high enough, so to speak. Especially in the beginning. This will only help you later on in your practice.

Although we won't be talking about Buddhism specifically many of these techniques have rich Buddhist histories. The first rule of Buddhism is morality. It's the first and last teaching. You don't have to convert to Buddhism (I don't consider myself Buddhist) but beware – if you aren't good to both yourself and others, if you're carrying around a lot of anger or guilt then you will have a hard time clearing your mind. We will deal with this in part with some specific solutions to common problems but first things first: be a good person. You don't need to read sutras or be religious. Be kind to others, treat yourself well and everything else will fall into place. This rule is crucial to your mindfulness success.

**Do not practice these techniques while you're driving or operating any kind of machinery.** At times these can be very powerful and deeply relaxing, altered states. You may find yourself pretty blissed-out after a session. Please use extreme caution when practicing. Also, if you have any health-related issues please consult your physician before undertaking these practices.

Last rule. Enjoy yourself. In a way, this goes back to Rule #3. This practice is meant to make life better with less suffering. Have fun and enjoy this internal adventure.

## Chapter 1: What Is Type A Behavior?

The human race is made up of an amazing variety of people. No two persons behave alike despite sharing most of their genetic makeup. It makes us humans the most complex of the earth's species. This age-old fascination has led to considerable study into the mysteries of human behavior.

Pioneering studies on Type A individuals were conducted by two American cardiologists Meyer Friedman and R.H. Rosenman. This was based on their observation of patients who came to them with heart conditions. A very unusual thing was noticed by an upholsterer who was called in to repair the waiting room chairs. He noticed that unlike normal wear and tear on the armrest and the backs of the chairs, only the front part of the chairs in their waiting room was worn out. An innocent comment by the worker got the doctors thinking and they made an interesting observation that some of their patients were extremely restless and tense while awaiting their turn in the waiting room. Their subsequent research shows that those patients displaying those anxious and tense patterns ran a greater risk of heart disease and elevated blood pressure levels than others. Earlier they were collectively termed 'Type A' personality. However, this is generally referred to as the Type A behavior pattern.

What is personality?

To understand behavior patterns, we must first know what constitutes 'personality'. It is the pattern of feelings, thoughts, behaviors and social adjustments which a person consistently exhibits over a significant period of time. This pattern greatly influences the person's expectations, values, and attitudes. It also affects his or her self-perception and predicts their reactions to other people, problems, and stress. Human behavior is made up of this complex network of thoughts and feelings. Needless to say, behavior is also influenced by the socio-cultural environment to which the person is exposed throughout his or her life.

Characteristics and Behavior

In the past fifty years, the term Type A has become a household phrase. It is loosely used to describe an extremely determined, rigid, competitive and work-obsessed individual. A Type A person is a normal individual functioning at maximum speed. He or she thinks that the time period for a particular goal is very limited and hence the sense of urgency in every thought and action. That urgency can sometimes translate into impatience and even hostility towards others.

While there is some debate over the characteristics of the Type A individual, there is consensus over the theory that they cannot be boxed into a single category. There are varying degrees on the spectrum. Those with a higher tendency towards Type A behavior and those with a lesser tendency. However, the main characteristic upon which most experts agree is competitiveness.

Below is a broad description of the traits of the Type A individual:

1) **Exaggerated sense of urgency**. Type A's constantly feel that they are running against time and that their tasks are too great for the available time-frame. They are generally multi-taskers, they are impatient with delays and have a constant sense of urgency. They typically dislike standing in line or waiting their turn for an extended period. They tend to check the time regularly and they usually opt for a quicker pace even when a slower pace is more appropriate.

2) **Competitiveness.** They may view even the simplest of tasks as a competition. While they may not always openly engage their co-workers or friends in an open challenge, internally, they compare themselves and their efforts with others

continually. They hold themselves to high standards and can be extremely critical if they do not perform according to their own expectations. They will go to great lengths to achieve their goals, however, the sense of satisfaction or achievement is short-lived because they are usually already reaching for the next win.

3) **Hostility and Aggression.** Due to their sense of urgency, they can be rude and hostile to others. With their singular focus, they may often show little regard for others' feelings. Their tendency towards perfectionism and seeing others as rivals can make them easily irritated with others and lack compassion with what they perceive as another's failings or weaknesses.

4) **Physical indicators.** Due to their intense nature, they may show physical characteristics that are indicative of stress. A few of the signs would be a clenched or hard jaw, nail-biting, fidgeting or dark circles around the eyes.

5) **A constant state of 'high'.** Type A individuals are constantly alert. Their brain works overtime and as a result, they find it hard to unwind and sleep. When their physical activity reduces, they go on mental overdrive. They are continuously planning and strategizing and when things do not go according to their meticulous plans they can be highly distressed.

6) **Obsessive-compulsive behavior.** Most of the persons diagnosed with obsessive-compulsive disorders (OCD) show varying levels of Type A behavior patterns. However, the obsessive–compulsive actions of the Type A individual does not have to be a behavior that is considered socially unacceptable. For example, it can be an obsession with physical fitness. They may insist on physical workouts regularly pushing themselves to extreme levels, and even when ill. They get a deep satisfaction from the 'burn' as it feeds their need for accomplishment. This obsession with their

body can lead to eating disorders, more often seen in women.

7) **Emotional Deficiency.** Many Type A individuals may seem cold and insensitive. They put on a façade by covering up their emotions and exposing a hard outer shell. However, they prefer to project this image so they do not come across as weak. Another reason is to not be exposed as being sensitive and vulnerable.

Despite the long list of traits that may seem negative at first glance, it is important to recognize that there are also distinct advantages to having Type A tendencies. Persons with a Type A personality are more competitive, more goal-oriented, more focused and often more diligent in whatever they do. They are go-getters – while others may sit on the sidelines content to discuss an idea and consider every angle, the Type A person will dive in and take action often without consensus. Depending on the context, some actions of the Type A person can be considered to be reckless but when the results of their actions are positive, they are often hailed as decisive and even visionary. They are prone to make big moves which can either yield massive success or colossal failures.

In the present-day scenario, the generation born between the 1980s to early 1990s, popularly called 'Gen-Y' strongly feels that they must be more Type A in order to succeed. The competition is so great nowadays, that it may be partly true. However, merely possessing Type A qualities, does not guarantee success nor happiness. For Type A's to be successful and happy, they must be rational and intelligent. With this combination, one can perform regular self-analysis and make the necessary adjustments to ensure there is balance in the actions that are taken towards life goals.

## Chapter 2: History Of Mindfulness

Mindfulness is a generic and overarching term that can apply to various contemplative practices. There is much overlap between mindfulness and meditation, so attempting to distinguish the two is difficult.

Mindfulness has been practiced throughout the world and by all religions, though they may have used terms other than "mindfulness." An ancient practice dating back 2,500 years, it is believed that mindfulness was first practiced by the ancient indigenous people of India. With time, the practice of mindfulness would be adopted by the religions of Buddhism, Hinduism, Muslims, Daoism, Christianity and by the countries of Asia, India, Europe, and America.

In today's society, we make reference to mindfulness as though it was a commodity or as if it was some New Age or spiritual movement. In fact, the practice of mindfulness can be traced as far back as religion itself.

The following are comments on religions and quotes from prominent historical figures as they relate to mindfulness.

In Islam, the Prophet Muhammad is said to have practice mindfulness. Also, the five daily prayers, also known as salat, and the five pillars of faith, are based on mindfulness.

In Judaism, mindfulness is a basis for the religion, as exemplified by prayer before eating, the mindfulness that food is a gift.

In Hinduism, the realized master Shivabalayogi was quoted to say "All philosophy remains talk unless people practice sadhana (spiritual practice)."

In Lamentations 3:28 are the words "Let him sit alone and be silent Since He has laid it on him."

From Isaiah 30:15: "... in quietness and in confidence shall be your strength ..."

From Psalm 46:10: "Be still and know that I am God."

"Be happy in the moment, that's enough. Each moment is all we need, not more." Mother Teresa

"Perfection of character is this: to live each day as if it were your last, without frenzy, without apathy, without pretense." Marcus Aurelius, Meditations

"Those who are awake live in a state of constant amazement." Shakyamuni Buddha.

"Nothing is as important as this day." Goethe

It is believed that the practice of mindfulness began in the Hinduism tradition around 1500 BCE. In Hinduism, mindfulness was practiced through the practice of yoga. As time went on, other religions adopted mindfulness practices; however, mindfulness is most often associated with the Buddhist tradition, where is practiced through meditation and breathing exercises, known as Sati.

Sathipatthana is the state of achieving mindfulness.

**Chapter 3: The Benefits Of Mindfulness Meditation**

Why should you bother spending five to ten minutes each day improving your focus on the present moment? What is it about mindfulness meditation that will improve your life?

It is reasonable for anyone to be asking these questions. After all, no one should practice mindfulness meditation just because their friends are into it, or that famous people are doing it, or that it is such a big trend that it will finally allow them to use the hashtag Namaste on social media. The practice of this of mindfulness meditation can offer so much more.

Now that you have a clearer image of what mindfulness meditation is, you probably want to know the reasons why you should incorporate it into your busy schedule. In this chapter, you will get to know the scientifically proven benefits that mindfulness meditation can bring to the table.

## Studies Supporting Mindfulness Meditation

One of the main reasons why mindfulness meditation is so popular is the fact that many scientific studies can attest to its usefulness. Many research studies have pointed out a correlation between its practice and the improvement of one's general well being.

For instance, it has shown promise in reducing anxiety, depression, and other clinically diagnosed mental disorders. It also aids in minimizing the mental disturbances many people suffer from each day, such as worry and stress.

Ever since the 1950s, many researchers have been delving into the topic of meditation. More recently, neurological scientists interested in the concept of mindfulness have been using digital instruments, such as the fMRI and the

EEG, to measure its effects on the human brain.

A recent study published in the **Journal of Psychosomatic Research** in 2015 focused on the mindfulness-based stress reduction for healthy individuals. The results showed that mindfulness meditation is moderately effective in reducing anxiety, distress, depression and stress, thus, improving the quality of life of the participants.

The year before that, a study published in the 2014 issue of **Psychosomatics**, explored the effects of mindfulness meditation practices in treating depressive disorders. The researchers concluded that there is significant scientific evidence to prove its positive effects on the physical and mental well being of patients who have clinical depressive disorders during the acute and sub-acute phases of their treatment.

Another study supports this claim, it was published in the 2014 issue of **JAMA Internal Medicine**, and commissioned by the US Agency for Healthcare Research and Quality. This study revealed that meditation helps minimize the negative effects of psychological stress experienced in multiple dimensions. The research recommends that meditation may be offered as a supplementary form of therapy to evidence-based interventions for people who are experiencing current anxiety or a depressive episode.

These studies are only part of a substantial body of evidence that supports the positive effects of mindfulness meditation. Its ever-increasing popularity continues to pave way for further research that will validate its relevance to a person's overall health and well being.

How Mindfulness can Improve your Life

Overall, scientific studies only seek to provide empirical evidence for the benefits that ancient practitioners of mindfulness meditation already know, accept and enjoy. Hopefully, you can also experience them for yourself. Dedicate a specific period each day to mindfulness meditation and you will surely notice a significant improvement in the quality of your own life.

Here are few of the benefits described by many practitioners:

Your brain becomes sharper.

The living brain is the most powerful and complex tool you have. What makes it so amazing is that it is highly adaptable to all the thoughts and behaviours that you do each day. For instance, by practicing certain behaviors and entertaining specific thoughts repeatedly, you train certain parts of your brain to chunk that information, thus, improving its development.

According to a study conducted by neuroscientist, Professor Richard Davidson, the consistent practice of **metta** meditation, a type of mindfulness meditation, which focuses on loving kindness, has tremendous effects on a person's ability to think positively. Other studies also prove that just practicing mindfulness meditation for short periods of time each day can already help improve your ability to focus.

This is great news for those who wish to become more productive and mindful of their daily tasks. For example, if you are a student who plans to study extensively for an important exam, you can practice mindfulness meditation in between breaks to help improve the ability of your mind to focus on what is in front of you. As a matter of fact, if you want to improve any skill in general, you will sharpen your brain through mindfulness.

You will learn to develop positive thoughts.

Negative thoughts are merely repetitive patterns in your brain called "rumination." Sometimes, they can also be in the form of experiential avoidance, or the process of avoiding certain thoughts that cause discomfort. Through mindfulness meditation, you can overcome these negative thinking patterns that will otherwise lead to depression and anxiety.

How does it do that?

First, mindfulness meditation helps you acknowledge the difficult experiences, feelings, or thoughts that you are experiencing. Through this acknowledgement, you begin your journey towards accepting them in a more curious and kind manner.

Through this practice, you turn into an observer of yourself, enabling you to see your negative thought patterns as if you are a third person looking in. In other words, you can take a step back from the chaos. You no longer become overwhelmed by your rapidly shifting thoughts and emotions but rather, you simply notice them.

Through these observations, you get the chance to understand yourself and your own habits better. Thus, you will realize that you have a choice, and that is to focus on what is healthy and right for you.

Your creativity and problem-solving skills will improve.

When the mind is trained to focus on the present moment, it eventually becomes increasingly receptive and positive, thus allowing you to create better solutions to the problems you face. In addition, your healthier state of mind will enable you to become more curious and open to possibilities, thereby leading to sharpened creative skills.

This is because mindfulness meditation unlocks your brain's ability to enter the state of "flow." Flow is described as the period wherein you are completely immersed in the task that you have right in front of you in an effortless way. Professional athletes, world-renowned artists, and bestselling writers claim to enter this state whenever they need to bring out their best creative and problem-solving talents.

You can experience deep relaxation each day.

Through the daily practice of mindfulness meditation, you can enjoy deep relaxation after a busy day at work free of charge. Aside from sleep, it is the best way to give your body and mind a rest from too many activities. However, it goes beyond the restful effect of sleep as mindfulness also gives you the opportunity to observe and appreciate the present moment, which will enhance and uplift your mood and thoughts.

Moreover, daily meditation will help enhance your brain's resilience to difficulties later on. This means you can cope with daily stresses more easily and ensure a clearer and more balanced mind in dealing with problems.

Your relationship with yourself and others will strengthen.

Taking the time to clear your mind of the mundane to become aware of who and what surrounds you in the present will definitely allow you to nurture an attitude of kindness and gratitude.

You can learn a lot from mindfulness, becoming aware of your body's natural ability to keep you alive, from paying attention to how your mind conjures thoughts and emotions, and from listening to the world around you. It makes you realize that nothing – including yourself – is permanent in this world. As each moment passes by, your life is also passing by. Noticing this can make anyone become more appreciative of who he or she is and who are special to him or her in life.

As you will soon find out, there are plenty of other benefits that you can gain from practicing mindfulness meditation. Some of these may be unique to you, while others may be benefits you share with others. However, regardless of the results, the practice is rewarding to your mind and body.

It is also important to note that mindfulness can be incorporated in each waking moment, not just during the time when you practice meditation. This is why, in the next chapter, you will find ways on how to apply mindfulness in your everyday life.

## Chapter 4: 21 Days Of Mindfulness

Before we start learning about mindfulness practices, we need to digress a bit, about how to be successful when introducing any change into your life. Mindfulness practice, like dieting or learning the French language, is easier if you have the right mindset.

Even with the same program in this book, some people will be amazingly successful and others will fail. The people who that will be successful exhibit the following six attributes:

The 6 success attributes

1. They ask themselves repeatedly: what is my motivation to practicing mindfulness? Better husband or wife; more present with my kids or friends; more focused at golf or work.

2. They don't let setbacks get them down for long. Mindfulness is tough. You will think it is not working; you will forget to practice and get down on yourself. Those

people who get back to it without beating themselves up too badly will do better.

3. They follow a process. They will commit to the actions recommended for the 21 days and beyond.

4. They believe. They can see themselves being successful and they remind themselves every day.

5. They look to constantly improve. If there is a technique that works better than another, they pay attention to that and focus more time there.

6. They don't practice haphazardly. in other words, there is quality in their actions, and they look to share mindfulness practices with loved ones who may be in need of this program.

Make it a daily habit of reviewing these attributes so you will stay with the program for the long haul; changing your brain's physiology takes at least three months. Your patience will be tested, particularly when you know you can introduce prescription drugs into your body and get that calmness you want in minutes. You also know that this option just dopes the monkey, it doesn't tame it.

That said, let us return to mindfulness. As a skill you will need to practice for the rest of your life, this practice will become as habitual as brushing your teeth. It takes minimum 21 days to introduce that habit. The goal of this chapter is to tell you what you need to do for the next three weeks to make mindfulness part of your daily routine.

*How to Make Mindfulness a Part of Your Life*

For the next three weeks, you are going to have to carve out a small amount of time each day to practice mindfulness. I suggest that you set aside a minimum of 30 minutes per day for mindfulness; if that is too difficult for you, practice for less time. The point is to practice daily.

Some of the mindfulness practices we will talk about in this chapter are things you can practice anywhere. Mindful breathing is a good example. The techniques I will describe are ones you can use when you are in a meeting at work or stuck in traffic on the way home. Other practices, such as mindful meditation and mindful eating, will require you to set aside some quiet time when you will not be interrupted.

The most important thing you need to do to make mindfulness a habit is to commit to time for it. Like any skill in life, the more you practice mindfulness, the easier it will be to use it. It will become second nature to you.

Mindfulness Exercises

Mindful Breathing

Mindful breathing is the simplest and most ancient form of mindfulness. It is something you can do in any situation. People who experience stress and anxiety say that a few moments of breathing mindfully can bring them back into their bodies in a positive way. Here are four basic techniques you can use.

Box breathing . Box breathing is the simplest and most straightforward of the mindful breathing techniques. Start by breathing out, emptying your lungs. Then breathe in for four counts, hold your breath for four counts, breathe out for four counts, and hold your breath for four counts. Each element of this breathing technique represents the 4 sides of a box. Repeat four or five times until fully present.

Counting breaths . The next technique takes a bit longer but it can be very helpful. Start by breathing out, emptying your lungs. Breathe in for one count and out for one count. Next, breathe in for two counts and out for two counts. Continue all the way up to ten, then settle into a regular breathing pattern that is comfortable for you.

4-7-8 breaths . This last technique requires some concentration, but it can be extremely effective at relieving intense stress. To do it, start by breathing out fully, emptying your lungs. Next, breathe in fully for four counts. Hold your breath for seven counts, and then breathe out for eight counts. Repeat at least four times or until you have brought your attention to what is causing you stress.

5-Tap . Start by exhaling fully, then slowly tap a finger or thumb against your hand or thigh, whatever your hand is settled on. Focus only on the finger tap. Once the 5 tap is complete, breathe in fully. Repeat until you feel energized and present.

These techniques are extremely simple, yet powerful. You can practice them anywhere, and they are a quick and discreet way to calm yourself and bring your attention to the present moment.

Mindful Eating

Eating is something that many people do while thinking about something else. Or worse, they eat on the run, barely chewing their food.

Mindful eating is a very simple way to reconnect with your food. One of the best ways to practice it is to use a simple, whole food like an apple. To do this exercise, find a quiet place to sit where you will not be interrupted. Choose an apple that looks appealing to you.

■ Before you take a bite of the apple, look at it and observe the color of the skin. Feel the weight of it in your hand. Sense the smooth texture of its skin beneath your fingertips.

■ Bring the apple to your nose and smell it. Think only about the way it smells.

■ Take a bite. Pay attention to the way your teeth feel when they puncture its skin, and the way the juice tastes in your mouth.

■ Chew the bite, noticing the texture of the apple's flesh and how it changes as you chew it. How does it feel as you swallow it?

■ Continue eating, noticing how your experience changes as you continue to eat. The juice that seemed very tart when you took your first bite may seem less so as you eat more.

■ Think about the fact that the apple grew on a tree and the journey it must have taken to get to you.

The purpose of this exercise is to take a moment and think about your food **as food**. Your body needs nutrition, including the nutrients contained in apples, to be healthy. Food is meant to be savored, and this exercise will help you remember how to do that.

Mindful Walking

Walking is another daily activity that we tend to take for granted. We let our minds wander as we walk, barely noticing where we put our feet or how it feels to walk. Using the same principle that we used for mindful eating, mindful walking is a way of reconnecting with a simple activity.

■ As you prepare to walk, take a moment to breathe. Deep breaths that fill your lungs with air will supply oxygen to your muscles.

■ Appreciate the way your feet feel in your shoes, and how they hug the ground.

■ Take a step, rolling your foot from heel to toe as you do. Let your arms swing freely. Notice the feeling of the ground beneath your feet.

■ Continue walking. Keep your attention focused on the actions you take as you walk – the way your feet move, the way your knees bend, and the way your lungs work a little bit harder to give your body the oxygen it needs.

■ If you wish, you can use your walk to notice the things around you: the leaves on the trees, a passing dog, or the warmth of the sunlight on your face.

■ If you feel your mind wandering, gently bring it back to your feet as they touch the ground.

You can walk as long as you wish, but it is best to do this exercise for a predetermined amount of time or distance. For example, you might want to mindfully walk during a morning break at work. You can apply the same principle to any other simple physical activity, such as swimming or riding a bicycle.

Mindful Meditation

The final mindful exercise I want to tell you about is mindful meditation. I will give you a few simple variations to try.

1. The first form of meditation is the simplest. Find a quiet place to sit where you will not be interrupted. Sit in a tall posture (slouching will make you sleepy). Start with some simple box breathing. Close your eyes, and continue to breathe evenly. You can continue with the box breathing or simply settle into a comfortable rhythm of even breathing. Focus only on your breath (at your nose, in your chest or at the belly). When you feel your mind wandering, and it will, bring attention to where your mind went and gently bring it back to your breath. Be kind

to yourself when your mind wanders; it always will. Be patient.

2. A variation on this simple meditation is to use a visual focal point to help keep you in the present moment. Some people find it helpful to light a candle and fix their eyes on it, or you may prefer to use a plant or flower. For this meditation, keep your eyes open. Breathe evenly and keep your focus on your visual focal point. When your mind wanders, bring attention back to your visual anchor.

3. Instead of a visual focal point, some people find it helpful to use a mantra – a short, meaningful phrase that they repeat with each breath. Pick any phrase that is meaningful to you and easy to say while breathing mindfully.

4. A fourth variation, one that requires a bit more effort, is a meditation with visualization. For this type of meditation, start with box breathing. When you close your eyes, instead of simply concentrating on your breaths, picture a tranquil spot

you love. Common choices include a beach, a forest, or a mountaintop. Visualize it as clearly as you can. Try to smell the air, see the sights, and feel the ground beneath your feet. Make your vision as complete as it can be. Alternatively, the Internet has an enormous volume of guided meditations where you listen to a soothing voice taking your mind's imagination to the place of your dreams.

It will be a big challenge to keep your mind focused on the present; that is normal. To better your chances of success, meditation practice will start off short and increase over the three week course.

The Counting Pyramid

Here's a way to kill two birds with one stone. Exercise & meditation all rolled into one.

Next time you go out for a walk, bike, or for run on a treadmill at the gym, instead of listening to music or a podcast, consider the following.

Imagine you are climbing a pyramid. Now, imagine it takes you one full breath in and out to climb one stair. See the image below. You are bounding up and down this pyramid effortlessly in your mind. In 5 breaths you are at the top 1-2-3-4-5. No rejoicing at the top! On the next breath, you climb down 4-3-2-1.

Try it now.

Keep yourself on track: visualize the number directly on the step of the pyramid as you count breaths. If you want a real work out, both mentally and physically, challenge yourself with a 200 step counting pyramid: 1-200 then 199-1. This will take you about 15 minutes or so.

When I started this technique, I often lost my place as my mind wandered. This is normal. When this happens, go back to the last number you remember counting and start again from there.

Consider making this part of your morning routine.

Wow! Exercising body and mind at the same time.

A Simple 21-Day Plan to Become More Mindful

Now it is time to talk about how to incorporate the above practices into your life and make them into a healthy and calming habit.

**Day 1** - When you first wake, review the 6 success attributes, then meditate for 5 minutes; use technique 1. Throughout the day, chose one of the four suggested mindful breathing techniques that might work best for you and pay attention to how it makes you feel. Throughout the day, use them when you feel stress, anxiety, or regret. Challenge yourself to use this technique at least once every hour – even a few focused breaths will suffice. Be kind to yourself if you forget. Remember, you are trying to instill a habit that is not there yet.

**Day 2** – When you first wake, review the 6 success attributes, then meditate for 5 minutes; use technique 2. Use the mindful breathing throughout the day when stressed and at least once every hour.

**Day 3** – When you first wake, review the 6 success attributes, then meditate for 5 minutes; use technique 3. Use the mindful breathing throughout the day when stressed and at least once every hour.

**Day 4** – When you first wake, review the 6 success attributes, then meditate for 5 minutes; use technique 4. Use the mindful breathing throughout the day when stressed and at least once every hour. Set aside 5 minutes to practice the mindful eating technique with the apple.

**Day 5** – When you first wake, review the 6 success attributes, then meditate for 5 minutes; choose the technique you prefer. Note: You should vary the techniques occasionally to keep the sessions as fresh as possible. After three months, you may feel that one or two methods work best for you. Use the mindful breathing throughout the day when stressed and at least once every hour.

**Day 6** – When you first wake, review the 6 success attributes, then meditate for 5 minutes; choose the technique you prefer. Use mindful breathing as needed and at least once every hour. Plan a minimum 10 minute mindful walk.

**Day 7** – When you first wake, review the 6 success attributes, then meditate for 5 minutes; choose the technique you prefer. Use mindful breathing as needed and at least once every hour. Plan to mindfully eat when you are alone and you can focus on the food.

**Day 8** – When you first wake, review the 6 success attributes, then meditate for 10 minutes. Use mindful breathing as needed and at least once every hour. Pay careful attention to what you eat at least one time during the day, even if you are in the company of other people.

**Day 9** – When you first wake, review the 6 success attributes, then meditate for 10 minutes. Use mindful breathing as needed and at least once every hour. Plan 15 minutes of exercise, walking or whatever you choose, and give it your full attention while you do it.

**Day 10** – When you first wake, review the 6 success attributes, then meditate for 10 minutes. Use mindful breathing as needed and at least once every hour. Mindfully eat at breakfast.

**Day 11** – When you first wake, review the 6 success attributes, then meditate for 10 minutes. In addition, take at least five minutes during the day to be fully present in whatever you are doing, whether it is washing dishes or playing with your kids.

**Day 12** – When you first wake, review the 6 success attributes, then meditate for 10 minutes. Use mindful breathing as needed and at least once every hour. Use mindful eating for breakfast, lunch, and dinner today.

**Day 13** – When you first wake, review the 6 success attributes, then meditate for 10 minutes. Use mindful breathing as needed and at least once every hour. Do a 15 minute walking meditation outside. Mindfully eat all your meals.

**Day 14** – When you first wake, review the 6 success attributes, then meditate for 10 minutes. Use mindful breathing as needed and at least once every hour. If you have not yet attempted the visualization technique, try it today. Mindfully walk and mindfully eat at least once today.

**Days 15 to 21** - For the final week of the plan, continue to review the 6 success attributes and meditate for 20 minutes first thing in the morning. You should also customize your mindfulness practice to incorporate the things that you find to be the most helpful. I strongly recommend building in a mindfulness routine that becomes as familiar as brushing your teeth.

By now, you should be feeling a big difference in your stress levels. Every day, use the mindful breathing techniques when you experience anxiety or stress. If you want some variety, try mindful play with your children, mindful vacuuming, or mindful grocery shopping.

**Beyond 21 days** - Continue your morning ritual. If the breathing technique is not habitual during the day, deliberately schedule it into your day until the habit is formed. Choose at least one activity a day where you pay attention to your moment to moment experience. Do this without judging, but with a mindset that allows you to see it for what it is. Allow yourself to be curious about what you think, what you feel emotionally or what your senses tell you.

**Chapter 5: The Need To Know**

Ignorance isn't bliss – it's fatal! Many people die due to reasons that could've been avoided – such as vehicular accidents, terminal illnesses, or accidental killings – had they known such clear and present dangers. A teenage driver gets killed when he drove past a red light in a major intersection in the early hours of the morning, not knowing there was a speeding Mack truck crossing the intersection. A woman didn't know that lumps in the breast aren't normal and by the time she finds out it's a symptom of breast cancer, she's already at Stage 4. Had the teenager and the woman known otherwise, they would still be alive today.

If you want to live a full life by beating depression, stress, and anxiety, you need to be aware of what causes or aggravates them – stressors. Here are the most common stressors you may already be encountering on a regular basis:

**Not Enough Time:** When you regularly strive to finish tasks that are urgent with not enough time, you will no doubt feel stressed and anxious! You should know – if you still don't by now – that stress has been scientifically established to cause many sicknesses and diseases, some of which are deadly or fatal.

**Unhealthy Lifestyle:** A lifestyle characterized by habits like binge eating, no exercise whatsoever, smoking, excessive alcohol consumption, and not getting enough sleep is one that can no doubt make you feel, anxious, stressed, and depressed. Why? It's because such a lifestyle is sure to make you suffer from major sicknesses or diseases later on and such conditions will definitely rob you of your peace of mind. Getting seriously sick can compound whatever stress, anxiety or depression you may be feeling, which leads to more sicknesses and…you get the drift.

**Too Many Things On Your Plate**: When you take on too much work, responsibilities or activities, it will render your previously enough time practically insufficient. And when you're chronically out of time, you'll experience chronic stress and consequently, sicknesses. Unless you're able to manage or rein in the amount of responsibilities you accept and activities you participate in, you're putting yourself at high risk for chronic stress.

**Unreasonable Expectations:** Another surefire way to be chronically stressed, anxious or worse, depressed, is to regularly set unreasonable expectations, regardless if it's expectations of you or of others. By virtue of being unreasonable, such expectations have a very low – even no – chance of ever being met. The more unmet expectations you have, the more you'll feel anxious, stressed or depressed.

**All Work And No (Or Little) Rest:** All work and no rest don't just make Jack a tired boy - it also makes him a very anxious, stressed or depressed one! Not being able to get enough rest – particularly sleep – will render you unable to recover well enough to take on the next day, having less than the required energy. Lacking sleep – and consequently energy – consistently makes you a very ideal candidate for chronic stress that will eventually lead to or aggravate anxiety, stress, sickness, or depression.

HOW TO BEAT YOUR STRESSORS

Simply doing nothing, going with the flow or living on autopilot won't help you manage or overcome your stressors and consequently, keep you from living your life to the full. By not owning your personal stressors, they will own you! That's why you have to take control, primarily by living your life with awareness and purpose! In other words, living life with mindfulness! Purposefully practice the art of mindfulness on a regular and consistent basis and you'll be able to experience how it feels to have your life's busyness and challenges become less and less able to stress you out, make you feel depressed, or give you anxiety. The more you experience this continuously weakening grip on your life, the more you'll get closer to living a full life.

In the next few chapters, we'll talk about the different ways you can practice mindfulness on your way to winning over anxiety and depression.

## Chapter 6: Finding Your Focus

The key to finding your focus is digging deep into yourself to find what it is you care about most. What are your innermost hopes, dreams, and values? This will not be a quick and easy project, but most likely, you already have some inkling as to what that is.

Many alternative practitioners, like healers and seers, believe in the mythical Third Eye. While invisible to the naked eye, the space just between your eyes in the center of your forehead is said to hold the key to unlocking our inner wisdom, from our divine selves, harnessing the power of the universe. While somewhat mystical, it actually corresponds with the very real, physically existent pineal gland. While all of its functions are yet to be discovered, it has been shown to be primarily responsible for sleep patterns and self-awareness.

For now, we can use the mystical concept as a means for getting in touch with our inner spirit, what holds the truth behind all of our deepest desires. Tapping into this potential will allow you to discover your most essential dreams and values. We all are given an idea of what we should stand for by following the lead of those around us. We are generally nice and law-abiding as our forefathers did, and that is the structure society gives us.

What sets us apart from others are the individual things we hold dear. Because the pull of society and work and family are so strong, it is very easy to ignore the cues and directives of our inner spirit. If you have ever felt your conscience nagging at you, you can recognize the influence of your inner spirit.

What are the benefits of letting your inner spirit take the reins and guide you? Trusting your instincts and following your passions will absolutely transform your life. In a physical sense, you will be doing things on a daily basis that bring you happiness and joy. On a spiritual plane, you are taking advantage of a whole new level of energy that will guide your life.

If you're thinking this all sounds a little far-fetched, you are probably not alone. How do you even get in touch with your inner spirit? We will discuss how to do this in a bit more detail later in this book, but let's take a look at some concrete examples for the power this has.

After you have found what you want to focus your life around, things will simply start coming together. When you are in a good flow of energy, everything seems to work out in a concerted effort. You don't really struggle with much, as you actually enjoy the new challenges that are entering your life. This can easily be explained in a work-career scenario. Let's look at Jessica's story:

Throughout her early twenties, Jessica took a job at her local pharmacy. After several years working minimum wage at a local deli, just next door to this pharmacy, the prospect of making just a dollar more per hour above her current rate excited her. This job brought her opportunities, although it wasn't really in her field of study. Jessica took these jobs part-time while she was a full-time student of nutrition.

For the next five years, Jessica worked up the ranks at this pharmacy, receiving small pay raises for each year she continued to work. In this time, she had graduated college and purchased a home with her husband. They started to build a life. Jessica was so afraid that she was going to lose everything, all of her work decisions from that moment forward were based on money.

When the pharmacy raises started to lose their luster, she looked for jobs in her studied field of nutrition. After finding a job of comparable salary in her field, she decided to take a higher-paying job working for a generator repair company.

Obviously, against her true passion. Being deeply embedded in her financial situation, Jessica certainly did not see this.

The next couple of years were miserable. She worked at a job she hated just for the money, meanwhile daydreaming of counseling clients and giving nutrition advice, the reason she studied nutrition in the first place. Her degree fell short of the qualifications to become a registered dietitian, her original goal. She told herself that she didn't need to have this title to be happy and successful, and this got her by for some time.

Unfortunately, after years of unsettled, unhappy jobs, her conscience got the best of her. The subtle hints and signals that went largely unignored for a number of years had finally become signs and symptoms. She gained weight, developed health problems, she fought with her husband, pushed people away, dreaded going to work in the morning. These were not symptoms of a normal life, but of her inner spirit dying.

Then the opportunities started to present themselves. A contact from an old friend in her field. This became a job offer for more money, and a job she had dreamed of. From there, an opportunity to finish her degree and become a registered dietitian. Embedded in all of that was the opportunity to live with a clean, satisfied conscience. She was doing what she dreamed of most, living the life that completely jived with her inner self.

Guess what? The signs and symptoms disappeared. The negativity washed away. In that process, she learned that she needs to trust her intuition, those nagging negative thoughts that are meant to deter from walking the wrong path. Today, she uses that intuition to guide her practice. She works freelance as a dietitian, taking jobs that appeal to her, and truly deciding what to do based on how it feels. Even better? The financial worries she once had all seem to work themselves out. The fun jobs seem to pay well, and when one job ends, something inevitably comes up.

Focusing on the needs and wants of your inner self will transform your life. Find that focus and run with it and everything will work out the way it is supposed to. Also, keep an open mind as to what your life should look like. Our physical brains often have a good picture of what life should look like, but you will find that following your happiness and values is much more fruitful than the big house and white picket fence.

## Chapter 7: Meditation Techniques For Beginners

Meditation is one of a more formal technique of achieving mindfulness than those that were discussed in the previous two chapters. Meditation is known to reduce stress and anxiety and that is an almost irrefutable fact. You don't need studies and outcomes of research programs to understand this. You can yourself try this out. Take the simplest form of meditation technique listed here and practice for about two weeks consistently and notice how much better you get at handling stress and anxiety than before.

Meditation is nothing but a technique to bring balance into your lives. As the ability to create balance in our lives increases, the benefits of meditation will unfold. Even in daily life, there are many forms of work and/or exercise which are nothing but an act of meditation. For example, a mother loving holding and cuddling her child is enjoying an act of meditation as love flows between the two lives. An athlete focused on completing his or her exercise regimen is an act of meditation.

Meditation is, therefore, an attempt to keep out external and internal distractions and focus on one activity with intensity and deep concentration. Therefore, even the activities discussed in the previous chapters on eating, walking, working, conversing, etc. are all forms of meditation. Meditation techniques help you achieve mindfulness. This chapter is focused on a more formal approach to the subject and includes some simple and easy-to-follow meditation methods. We will start with some tips on how to get started on meditation.

Tips to Get Started on Meditation

Find a quiet place and time – This is the first and foremost thing you need to do before starting off with any meditation technique. Find a place and time where you will not be disturbed for about 15 minutes. Initially, this duration of time is sufficient. But, as you get better at meditation, you will find yourself being able to hold the meditative state for a longer time.

Position yourself comfortably – While sitting cross-legged on a mat on the floor is the ideal position, feel free to sit in a chair in a comfortable position too. Ensure your back is straight and it would be great if you don't have any back support. However, if you do have a back problem, feel free to find a seating position that is most comfortable for you. You have to remain physically as stable as possible during the meditation time. Keep your hands on your thighs/legs with the palms facing upward.

Become completely present in the 'now' – Be aware of your present surroundings. Where are you sitting? What can you hear? How does it feel to sit the way you are sitting? Are your shoulders sagging or are you sitting in a rigid manner? Are you relaxed? What are the thoughts running through your mind? Don't react to anything. Simply observe. If there is any discomfort in the way you are seated or positioned, this is the time to get comfortable.

Pay attention to your breath – Without making any effort to control how you breathe, simply pay attention to your breath. Observe the way air gets in through your nostrils. Then, as you breathe out, feel the breath coming out of your nostrils. Do not try to control the speed of your breath. Breathe as you normally would. Simply watch and observe the entire breathing in – breathing out cycles. Your mind will wander. Let it wander; but, gently pull it back to your breath.

Pay attention to your body movements - Feel your stomach and chest area expanding as you inhale. Similarly, when you exhale, feel your stomach and chest area deflate as the air goes out of your system. Focus on each part of your body and as you focus, observe how you feel there. Start from your toes and move gradually to the top of your head, stopping at each point to observe the sensations in that part.

Practice and practice more – Like everything else in the world, perfection can be achieved only through practice. Start with even 5-minute duration for daily meditation and slowly increase it to what you are comfortable each day. This is the simplest form of meditation you can use. Feel free to start off immediately and persist in your efforts and watch the positive differences in your life.

More Meditation Tips for Beginners

Meditation is not magic. It is a small way of opening your mind to bigger horizons than before. It is a small way to begin looking at yourself in a manner you have never done before. Meditation is 'me time' when you focus on your thoughts and follow them as they ebb and flow without being disturbed by anything else. The following tips are meant to help you get started and remain as committed as possible in your meditative journey.

Sit for only 2 minutes – While on the face of it, this might seem ridiculously easy, sit for two minutes doing nothing and then decide if it is easy or not. If it is easy for you, increase the initial duration to 5-15 minutes. If you think 2 minutes itself is too much, then let this be your initial period of meditation. You can increase it gradually over a period of time. Starting small is the most effective way of achieving success.

Finish your meditation session in the morning itself – We are simply talking not more than 15 minutes for the first 2-3 months. This time can be easily accommodated in the morning itself. The reason why the morning is better is once the day begins and you get into the daily routine, meditation will simply fly out of your head. So, do it first thing in the morning. In fact, name your waking alarm as 'do meditation,' as a form of a reminder for yourself.

Don't worry about the technique – simply get into the act – Avoid thinking that only if you get the technique right, that meditation is going to be useful. There is nothing like this. Forget about the technique. Just sit down for 2 minutes and get into the act. Don't worry about which cushion to use. Quit thinking about which dress to wear. Simply sit in a chair comfortably and pay attention to your breath. That's it.

Focus on your emotions – As you settle down in your meditation position, observe your emotions. How are you feeling? Are you anxious, worried, tense, feeling nothing, tired? Remember whatever emotion you bring in to the meditation session is perfectly fine. Soon you will know and realize the temperate nature of all emotions; good and bad.

Count your breaths initially – This will help you focus your mind on the meditation session. Count 1 as you breathe in. Count 2 as you exhale and so forth. Repeat this count until 10 and start again from 1.

Gently bring back your wandering mind – Your mind will wander and your thoughts will go around the world; to your cousin in New York to your sibling at home to your newfound Facebook friend in some remote corner of Africa and more. Your thoughts will go everywhere with gay abandon. There is no problem with that. Go with your thoughts and gently bring them back to your breath and start counting from 1 again.

You are bound to feel frustrated initially. It's a perfectly fine reaction. Everyone goes through it. Simply persist, follow your thoughts, smile at yourself, and bring your mind back to the meditation session. You will find success if you persist. It is in the nature of your mind to come back to the present, remember?

Develop a love for your thoughts – Your thoughts are part of you. Love them as you would love yourself. Look at the thoughts that come up during your meditation session as friends. Don't treat them as intruders or your rivals. They are part of yourself although they are not your entire self. Don't be harsh with them. Gently guide them to where you want them to go.

Quit worrying about doing things wrong or not getting the technique right – There are no right and wrong ways to the flow of your thoughts. They will keep flowing and you will have to simply nudge them back to the present. Another thing to keep in mind is that meditation is not meant to clear your mind of thoughts. It is meant to help you manage your thoughts in a more productive way than before.

Moreover, we cannot clear our mind of thoughts because thoughts are the basic elements of the mind, at least to the extent our five senses knows it to be. Yes, there are people who have achieved higher levels of consciousness by 'clearing' their mind, it seems. Our meditative sessions are not meant for that. Only try to pay attention to the present moment. Meditative sessions are designed to help you with just that.

Remain with the thought that comes up – While gently getting your thought back on the meditative focus is one way of handling disturbing thoughts, another way is to stay with the thought that arises until it ebbs and disappears. Just like how you handle negative emotions (spoken in an earlier chapter), observe the thought that comes up in your mind in a non-judgmental manner with an air of curiosity. This will help you relieve some of the anger and frustration you feel when thoughts keep coming to disturb your meditation.

Meditating through a body scan – In addition to focusing on your breath, you can look at a meditative session that does a body scan. Nearly all the meditative techniques that are popular work with some or all parts of the body ranging from breathing to eating to walking. Mindfulness involves a lot of thought to the sensations that take place in your body at any moment in time. So, body scan meditation is a great technique that will help you improve your mindfulness attitude immensely as you practice focusing on and observing each body part in turn. Here's how body scan meditation works.

Lie on your back with your legs apart and your arms a little away from your body. Feel free to cover yourself with a blanket if the temperature is cool. Moreover, it is possible for the body temperature to drop a bit during the session. Therefore, it does make sense to cover yourself with a blanket.

Let go of all your feelings and become aware of your inner self. Just remain lying down and allow the thoughts to flow. Go with your thoughts for a little while and watch them dissolve into new ones.

Focus on your breath for a few counts

Now, move your attention from your breath to your toes. Simply feel the sensation in your toes and observe it. If you cannot feel anything, then simply observe the lack of sensation in your toes.

Slowly, move your attention from your toes to your feet, ankle, calves, knees, thighs, the pelvic area, your stomach, chest, shoulders, the upper arms, forearms, hands, and fingers. Then move your attention to your neck upward to your lips, nose, eyes, ears, forehead, and the top of your head.

Each time your mind moves off to another thought, follow it for some time, observe the thought, and gently bring back the mind to the body scan and continue from where you left off.

As you process each part, imagine the oxygen from your breath being filled in that particular part. Notice and observe the sensations at each part too.

When you have finished the entire body scan, imagine your breath is sweeping your entire body from head to toe as you breathe in and from toe to head as you breathe out. This sensation of the breath will help you relax.

In the last 1-2 minutes simply focus on being. Don't do anything. When thoughts come, follow them until they merge into the next one. Follow the second one until it merges into the 3rd one and so forth.

With practice, this entire exercise can be a very nourishing experience for your body and mind.

Finally, the most important aspect of meditation and mindfulness is to remain committed to your endeavor. It is not going to be easy. Yet, the results of success are great and sustaining. So, don't give up. Simply persist and achieve your meditative end. Keep growing as a person.

**Chapter 8: What Are Negative Emotions?**

While still appreciating the goodness of mindfulness, we must factor in the negative emotions. Social media has been a very good avenue to hide one's true emotions. Everyone pretends to be happy in their posts. But since we are human beings, there's no way we can avoid having these negative emotions from time to time, and this ends up making us sad.

As we're trying to understand negative emotions, let's look at it from the opposite direction, that is, positive emotions. Positive emotions are positive feelings like joy, love, interest, and contentment. All of these are coming from desirable situations. So we can safely state that a negative emotion is any intense negative feeling or emotion that transmits profound surges of stress hormones through our body.

There's no contention about it; anger, frustration, shyness, fear, envy, guilt, helplessness, hopelessness, loneliness, ego, and of course, the inferiority complex, among others, are undoubtedly negative emotions. Unfortunately, if we take the phrase "negative emotions" grammatically, we may miss a very vital point, because we shall be emphasizing the word" negative" as the opposite of the word "positive". However, "negative" emotions have a lot of positives in them.

An article entitled, "Beyond Happiness: The Upside of Feeling Down" written by Matthew Hutson for the publication **Psychology Today,** posits that even though they're referred to them as negative, they are not necessarily negative in their impact on our lives. And being truthful to their semantic connotations, negative emotions can, through their weight on our mind, immobilize, demoralize, or even paralyze us. They can actually have worse effects on us, especially during critical times that are difficult to deal with.

However, they don't have to be if handled mindfully. According to Huffington's article entitled "How to Turn Negative Emotions into Your Greatest Advantage" negative emotions can be a blessing in disguise. They help us spot where our problem lies and show us how to fix it. He goes as far as saying that negative emotions can serve as a catalyst for positives, aiding our positive realizations. That would be if we handle them well.

So, negative emotions are more beneficial than you might imagine. As we discuss the effect of negative emotions on us, let's begin to see them as somewhat beneficial and not totally inimical.

The Impact of Negative Emotions on People

Have we indirectly painted only positive pictures of negative emotions? By no means! As you revert to the point we made on negative versus positive emotion on page 19, you will see negative emotions as they should be seen.

Scores of psychologists, psychiatrists, and social scientists specialized in various fields have not stopped spending millions of dollars researching the beneficial side of the negative emotions like sadness, guilt, pessimism, anger, anxiety, and jealousy. What they have come out with shows that they can be a driving force for good in our lives and that positive emotions are not characteristically behavioral.

Have the above points deeply entrenched in your mind as we look at both sides of the coin in analyzing next the effects of some of these negative emotions.

### Anger

Research has shown that youth who are usually angry are two to three times more at risk of developing metabolic syndrome, which is a dangerous precursor to various forms of heart diseases. **Daily News** of New York once reported, "Men prone to angry tantrums or sulky hostility are more likely to develop an irregular heart rhythm called atrial fibrillation." We can go on and on to itemize the debilitating effects of the negative emotion called anger.

Some of the responses to anger at work can be explosive outbursts, thoughtlessly quitting the job or threatening to do so, or some other irrational behavior. The anger itself might be triggered by the conflict between coworkers or between an employer and an employee. It can also be caused by frustration or a feeling of unfair and unjust treatment.

But to keep your anger under control, you need to mindfully take yourself out of the situation and allow yourself to cool down. You'll soon realize, when your anger has subsided, that there are more mature ways to deal with the situation or the action that caused the provocation.

### **Envy**

Envy has been defined as "the painful or resentful awareness of an advantage enjoyed by another, accompanied by a desire to possess the same advantage." Just like any malignant growth, envy can take over your life and destroy your happiness.

According to the **Encyclopedia of Social Psychology**, people envy those they consider their equals in age, experience, social background, or in some other way. For instance, a salesman might not envy a famous sports star; but the success of a fellow salesman may produce this emotion in him.

And equity theory puts it that we're bound to be motivated by a sense of fairness or equity. On the positive side, the resulting envy can move us to intensify our efforts at work so that the rewards of hard work, like an increase in pay or promotions, can be ours.

It's when the rewards are not forthcoming or are not commensurate to our efforts that envy develops along with other negative feelings.

The encyclopedia mentioned earlier recommends that you must first identify envy's hostile nature. Genuine humility and modesty will enable you to appreciate and have the positive estimate of whatever abilities and good qualities others possess. If you avoid the situation that produces envy in you and by all means desist from an unnecessary comparison of yourself with others, envy will not get the better of you.

### Fear

Fear is a very powerful emotion, so strong that it is capable of ruining one's happiness, robbing one of hope, and destroying one's reasoning. It has been said to be more destructive than the worst ever physical malady. No wonder fear has been aptly described as a mental poison.

As a matter of fact, fear has affected the way we live and the choices we make. There's the fear of losing one's job, fear of uncertainty. A hard-to-please supervisor or workplace bully, and other work place tensions can also heighten fear and distress at work. Nevertheless, you can allay the workplace fear or, at least, reduce it by constantly being on the lookout and constantly being the best at what you do. Always adjust your resume to fit your current status and be on the lookout for other employment opportunities. In that case, is fear as a negative emotion filled with nothing but all bad?

Again, what about the effect on your health? Living with fear can be very stressful. Depression and the damage it causes to a person's health cannot be overemphasized. A health magazine states that stress suppresses our immune system and can be a contributing factor in most fatal diseases. The magazine adds that our body, if overly exposed to fear, will develop symptoms of wear and tear. Depending on the organ affected mostly by fear, hypertension, heart disease, gastrointestinal disorders, ulcers, kidney disease, insomnia, headaches, depression, and anxiety disorder can develop.

**Guilt**

A renowned German philosopher, Friedrich Nietzsche, once said, "Guilt is the most terrible sickness that has ever raged in man." But is every feeling of guilt a negative emotion? Is it always bad? Other researchers don't think so. Dr. Susan Forward, a therapist and author who enjoys an international recognition, for instance, sees it differently. She says, "Guilt is an essential part of being a feeling, responsible person. It's a tool of the conscience."

If you have a sense of guilt because of unaccomplished assignments, or because you feel you're on the wrong side of an issue with a colleague, that feeling can hardly be a bad one. It's rather positive from a negative emotion, which can be a workplace motivator. It may move you to always strive to meet or exceed your demands and teach you how to mend up strained relationships.

**Helplessness**

This is another negative emotion that can paralyze people. It turns challenges into insurmountable problems. The ordinary work looms larger in your heart. A molehill can be turned into a tall mountain. All these are the effects of helplessness. It is usually confused with hopelessness. But they are slightly different in causes and effects. The feeling of helplessness at work may be a warning sign that should be heeded. It can tell you that you're overly concerned about your career or that your paths are not leading to the success you desire. It can also signal you that depression is knocking on the door. For the above reasons, it should not be seen only as a negative emotion, for it can be a force for good.

Practical tips for managing negative emotions through mindfulness

Although we have seen that negative emotions can have positive effects, they don't naturally do so. The effects are actually worse than we've mentioned so far, unless we manage them well. Negative emotions can take a great toll on our health.

Writing in **The Sacred Balance,** Davis Suzuki expresses this matter chemically. According to him, the condensed molecules produced by breath exhaled from verbal expressions of emotions like anger, hatred, and jealousy are full of toxins. To put it in perspective, the toxins are potent enough to snuff the life out of 80 guinea pigs if they continued to be exhaled for more than one hour. Our take from that? If negative emotions are not well-managed and processed into something positive, a lot of damage is being done to our body.

Have you ever experienced pains, tightness of chest, unexplained inflammation resulting in sores? What happened and how were you feeling just a few moments before you started having the experience? Analyze your emotion. Is it a positive or a negative one? You may not immediately connect any those negative emotions to what you're physically experiencing, because we're often not in touch with ourselves these hectic days. But the evidence does more than suggesting that this is the case.

Since we can't run away from negative emotions, and since their effects are real, let see how we can manage them and process them into producing positive effects. This is where mindfulness comes to our aid again. Taking into consideration the following ways, we can mindfully manage these negative emotions.

Pause and Look Within

As soon as you realize that you have some discomforting feeling, apply mindfulness. According to the practice, sit for a moment, take a deep breath, and try to become aware of everything happening within and around you. You will be able to identify the emotion, be it shame, guilt, anger, or fear, before it wreaks its havoc. Once you determine the emotion, you'll be better prepared to accept it and live with it, rather than trying to suppress it. As you are mindfully responding to the emotion, you will be enriching your life with new experiences and accomplishments.

Don't Deny the Emotion

Once you acknowledge that the emotion is in you, you'll be able to tame its effect. For instance, don't be shy to say, "I'm ashamed." Don't be too afraid to say, "I am feeling fearful." Say it to yourself first, and then to those who deserve to be told.

You're mindfully accepting that the emotion that is in you in itself is enough to calm and soothe you. It will fill you with compassion, rather than condemnation for yourself. As a response to that, you won't punish yourself; rather you will want to put yourself above the situation that brought you down.

When people say to someone experiencing a negative emotion, "be strong," "pull yourself together," they don't really know the full import of what they're saying. It's naïve to assume that someone can be stronger than his or her emotion. Rather than trying to reject or ignore the emotion, be mindfully open to it.

As you're trying to be open to it, you're creating a mental state around the emotion. You will be able to witness it run its course and leave a positive mark on you. Mindfulness will show you that you're not what you feel. Your emotion of the moment cannot define your totality.

*Remember That Emotions Are Ephemeral*

If it is true that tough times don't last, but tough people do, how much more so with emotions, which are quite transient. They are like mist appearing for just a day and disappearing tomorrow. Most times emotions don't live as long as the situation that triggered them. The emotion of guilt resulting from failing a test will soon fade away after you've realized that you have another opportunity to take the test again and you've realized the cause of your failure. But failure is still there.

We, unfortunately, take emotional surge personal. With mindfulness, however, we would see any emotion as a passing phase, as just a mental event in a fleet of events. That is the suggestion from Elisha Goldstein, a teacher of Psychology and Mindfulness. He recommends saying to ourselves, "While this is a temporary feeling, it is here right now. How can I care for it? What do I need?"

Investigate the Cause

After the passage of the phase of the blues, you will be able to dissect the negative emotion and pinpoint the harbinger, cause, or contributor. By taking such a look inwards, you're set to understand the cause of the emotion. You may find out that the emotion comes from unbridled thoughts. It could that some unwarranted worry about something or someone has gravitated toward the face of anxiety. A thoughtless word or action of someone around you (at work or at home) may have produced resentment that has spiraled to the point of anger or embarrassment. Something may have challenged your beliefs, values, and dented your societal expectation and judgments. By all means, mindfully dealing with negative emotion requires that you understand the cause.

Respond Appropriately

Know this fact: You can't definitely control other people's actions, but you can control your reactions. Once you always react negatively to negative emotions caused by an external agent, you're not the mindful type. Mindfulness will assist to determine if your thoughts are not adequate and if they should be jettisoned quickly. Through mindful meditation, you will know if all you need to do for now is to embrace the emotion. You can also see clearly if you have to up your effort in some areas to get a better result.

Resist the temptation to control your emotions

Since you now know that emotions are temporary, resist the urge to control them. Don't try to quicken the pace of negativity. On the other way around, don't attempt to hold on to the emotion for any reason. When you're mindfully dealing with a negative emotion, be open to the outcome. At times, you'll need to stay out of the picture and see how observers around you would conceptualize the issue. It is through a mindful way that you'll be able to manage your emotions without controlling them and letting them control you. Put everything in its place.

## Chapter 9: Mindfulness During Your Commute

If you are like most people then it is likely that you spend an hour, if not more, of your day commuting to and from work. Most people fill this time by listening to podcasts, cursing at their fellow commuters, catching a quick bite to eat, or, if they are less safety conscious, reading or shaving. While all of these things certainly help pass the time, they do little for their peace of mind or overall wellbeing. That's where practicing mindfulness meditation during the commute comes in as the repetitive nature of the drive is a perfect time to clear your mind and focus on achieving a state of mindfulness that will put other drivers to shame. By practicing mindfulness meditation on the road, you will find that you arrive at work ready to meet the challenges of the day head on, and arrive home at the end of the day with a clear head and heart, with the cares of the day left somewhere on the turnpike. Practicing mindfulness meditation on the go will allow you to reach your destination in a calm and focused state, that allows the stresses of rush hour traffic to fade into the background. What's more, practicing mindfulness meditation will also ensure you drive as safely as possible because you will be completely focused on the moment and the traffic that surrounds you.

Morning Commute

In order to make the most of your commute you are going to want to practice mindfulness from the very first moment that you enter your vehicle. As such, the first thing that you will want to do is to announce your intention aloud to the universe to help you get into the right mindset from the start. With your intentions made plain, the next thing that you are going to want to do (even before starting your vehicle) is to take several deep breaths. This will allow you to focus your attention on the sensations that your senses are providing you in order to ensure that you are in the right mindset even before you hit the road.

During this period, you want to take special care to focus on your body and the way it feels as you sit in your seat, the way your hands feel on the steering wheel and the way the world around you looks as you stare out at it from behind the windshield. From there, let the sensations of feeling expand outward and downward so that you feel your feet and the pressure you exert on the pedals before starting your vehicle.

As you begin your commute you are going to want to pay special attention to everything that is going on around you, both to the vehicles that you are directly interacting with as well as the people on the sidewalk and the buildings and signs that you previously passed without giving them a second thought. While this is going on be sure to also give some attention to your eyes as they are taking everything in and your ears as they convey the sounds of hundreds, if not thousands, of other people all moving together in relative harmony. Focus on these things, and only these things while you drive and you will be surprised at how much less of a hassle waiting in traffic suddenly becomes.

While this might initially strike you as too simple in order to produce the type of results you are looking for, it is important to put your doubts aside and give it a try before writing it off completely. Remember, when you first get started, even if you have already begun practicing mindfulness meditation in other facets of your life, it is perfectly natural for a stream of thoughts to be running through your head. This is especially true when heading into work as there are likely more things that you need to do than there are hours in the day to do them. Nevertheless, it is important to put everything else aside and strive to remain in the moment as thoroughly as possible.

For most people, the work day is a time for constant multitasking and this typically begins before the day itself does in the form of one form of electronic communication or another. As such, if you find that you are having a hard time focusing on the task at hand during your commute it may help to make a conscious effort to limit your electronic communication to a set period of time in the morning and ignore it for the rest of your morning until you have reached your destination and are ready to shift your day into high gear. While it may be difficult to ignore all of your notifications at first, after a few weeks you will wonder how you ever functioned when you were so closely tethered to your smartphone.

Suggestions to improve your morning commute

If you find it hard to get into the right mindset when the time comes to set off for work, consider working a few moments of mindfulness into your day as soon as you wake up. Use the first few moments of the day to stretch your senses, as it were, and try and take in as much information about your surroundings as possible.

Additionally, you may find it useful to take stock of the thoughts that are already running through your mind at this hour and consider how they may affect your morning both for good and for ill. Getting into the habit of running a pre-assessment will allow you to jump into the more productive aspects of mindfulness meditation as soon as you get in your vehicle.

When you find yourself thinking negative thoughts about the upcoming work day you may find it helpful to avoid banishing them as soon as they appear. Instead, you may want to try cognitively reframing whatever it is that you are thinking of in an effort to turn them around until you can view them in a more positive light. Not only will this help to make each day a little brighter, it will help you approach the day more confidentially and with prevent extra stress or anxiety from clouding your day before it even properly begins.

Use every moment of gridlock and every red light as a moment to quickly close your eyes, take a deep breath and to refocus on the task at hand. The frequent stop-and-go creates a natural barrier for thoughts that may have slipped through your mental blockade and will help to ensure that you stay on task no matter what else may have grabbed your attention. Remember, your goal during this time is to focus on what your senses are telling you to the exclusion of all else.

In order to ensure that your morning commute mindfulness session proceeds as smoothly as possible you are going to want to avoid thinking about work as much as possible, especially if something is going on that seems to naturally draw your attention. The pressures of the day can begin naturally building without you even realizing it, leaving you feeling beaten and worn down before the day even starts. Only by remaining vigilant can you stay focused on the moment in order to ensure that your day is ultimately as productive as possible. Taking the time to worry about problems that you can't solve until you get to work will gain you nothing and only make it more difficult for you to focus on the moment.

Evening Commute

While the goal of the morning mindfulness meditation commute is to focus your energy for the coming day, the goal of the afternoon mindfulness meditation commute is to provide you with an opportunity to relax and detox from the stress of the day to ensure that when you make it home your heart is light and your head is clear. When done properly it will ensure that the stress of the day has melted away entirely and that you are ready for whatever it is that the evening may throw at you. With enough practice, instead of dreading the evening commute and the barrier it represents between you and your free time, your evening commute will become a buffer between your happiness and the stresses of the outside world. Remember, practice makes perfect! Once you reach your vehicle, the first thing that you are going to want to do is to take an extra moment or two to think about the day that is coming to an end and any particular sticking points that may have unpleasant ramifications for the future. Consider why these incidents are sticking in out in your mind and what emotions they have attached themselves to and how you may be able to turn things around tomorrow. With your mental inventory complete, you will them want to make a conscious effort to let all of the negative emotions that you are holding on to float away on the mental breeze. While clearing your head you are also going to want to make a conscious effort to relax, starting with your neck and working your way down your entire body.

Next you are going to want to slowly take several deep breaths. As you do so you are going to want to focus on the feeling of the air as it enters your lungs, filling them until they are full to bursting. As you exhale you are going to want to visualize any stress you may have picked up throughout the day leaving your body as you do so. Visualize the air circulating through your body and consider how the motion makes you feel, use this practice as a gateway to considering the rest of your body and get back in touch with the sensations that the workday may have otherwise dulled. Focus on each of your senses in turn and let them bring you more fully into the moment piece by piece.

Once you have returned to a state of mindfulness, feel the pressure of the seat on your person, the feel of your hands on the steering wheel and the pressure exerted by your foot (or feet) on the pedals. As you drive you are going to want to remain in the moment as completely as possible, blocking out any thoughts that may still linger relating to the workday that you have not yet managed to shake.

However, when you find yourself stopped in traffic or waiting for a red light, instead of refocusing on the task at hand you are going to want to instead focus on the tension that the day has left in your body and focus exclusively on letting go of it and helping your body to relax. Each time you come to a stop you will want to focus on a different part of your body that you can feel holding onto the day's tension and visualize it leaving the body as you begin moving again. Once again you will want to start with your neck and work through your body all the way to the tips of your toes. If you make it through your entire body before you make it home then start again and repeat the process. When you finally reach your destination take an extra moment to consider how much better you feel now than you did before you left work and make one last effort to leave any workday complaints at the office where they belong.

*Suggestions to improve your evening commute*

While it is all well and good to try focus on leaving your negative thoughts at the office, it can frequently more difficult in practice than it is in theory. As such, if you find yourself clinging to a particularly negative thought despite your best efforts it is important to push it to the back of your mind instead of letting it drag down your entire commute and prevent you from reaching the state of mindfulness that you are aiming for. Failing to do so will only lead to an excess of tension that you will be unable to get rid of as your body follows your mind's lead. If you simply focus on your breathing and work at remaining in the moment as much as possible, nine times out of ten the thought will pass on its own.

If you find that you are still unable to get the negative thought or thoughts to subside and allow you to go on your way unmolested, you may find it useful to instead bring the full of your focus to bear on it in an effort to find out just why this thought continues to stick in your mind. In most cases you will find that the thought has actually gathered a greater amount of importance in your mind and that the reality of the situation isn't nearly as bad as your stress, nerves and anxiety have made it out to be.

With a little extra thought, you can often formulate a plan of attack against the negative thought to ensure that when the situation where you actually have to deal with it finally arises you are more than to handle it in the best and most efficient way possible.

If you are still having trouble letting the day go and regaining the state of mindfulness that you can more easily reach during your morning commute then you might find a mantra to be a good way to get your mind back on the right track. The following are common mindfulness mantras that can be useful in practically any situations:

May I understand my discomfort

May I discard my discomfort

May I be stress free, happy and anxiety free

The cares of the day are behind me

I am in charge of my own happiness

It is important to keep in mind that there is more than one way to practice mindfulness meditation and that what works for someone else might not work for you. Regardless of what you need to do in order to get into the proper mindset, if it helps you reach a state of mindfulness then it can be considered mindfulness meditation. The only time you need to worry about doing something wrong is if you use the fact that it can sometimes be difficult to find a state of mindfulness as an excuse to give up on the practice completely. Remember, practicing mindfulness is a long journey and it can take several months in order to truly understand yourself, don't get discouraged and keep up the good work.

## Chapter 10: Using Mindfulness To Overcome Anxiety

Anxiety, we all face it at some point in our lives, but there are those times when the anxiety becomes so intense we have no idea how to deal with it. Many times this can lead to anxiety disorders if we are not careful. Using mindfulness can help to prevent this.

There was a time when anxiety ruled my life. I was so afraid of everything that could happen, as well as what had happened. I focused all of my time preparing for what might happen instead of enjoying my life each day.

Those who are suffering with anxiety often report a large amount of fear in their lives, this causes the fight or flight response to kick into overdrive. They suffer from negative thinking. They often think the things that are happening are going to be a lot worse than what really occurs or they underestimate their ability to handle the situation.

Many doctors will teach people who are suffering from anxiety problems that they need to change the way they are thinking, but when you use mindfulness to overcome anxiety you accept the thinking as it is.

This may at first seem as if it is only going to make the issue worse. However, as time goes on and you practice mindfulness, you will be able to let your thoughts flow freely by acknowledging them without judging the situation. The more you practice, the more you will find that you are able to accept the situation as it is and allow yourself to move forward.

By remaining mindful, you are able to realize the anxiety you were suffering from was merely a reaction to what you perceived to be a threat.

Let's take a look at a situation of a young girl I know. She just had her first child and was already nervous about raising him on her own. This girls mother became very critical of her, wanting her to give the baby up. When the girl refused, the mother began telling the girl that she could not take care of the baby, that child protective services would take the baby away from her.

As time went on the girl began to believe what she was being told and was afraid to even put the baby down. She believed that someone was coming to take the baby whenever there was a knock at her door. She was unable to have a life or even hold a job due to the fear of leaving the baby with anyone.

Once she started practicing mindfulness, she had to learn that she was as a mother allowed to worry about her baby. She was allowed to experience all of the feelings that had caused her to suffer so much. The most important thing that she had to do was understand that what she was perceiving would happen if she answered her door or when to work was far worse than what would actually take place. It took quite some time working with this girl for her to completely understand that what her mother had caused her to believe was completely untrue.

Now you may be sitting there saying to yourself, that is all great but I didn't have someone telling me bad things were going to happen or that I couldn't handle the situation, but you would be wrong. Instead of having a parent like the girl did telling you that something awful is going to happen or that you can't handle what is happening, you are possibly the one telling yourself that.

We tend to believe ourselves much faster than we do when others tell us something. So simply telling yourself once or twice that you are unable to handle any given situation will do more damage than someone else telling you the same thing 10 times.

By using mindfulness and staying in the moment, you get rid of the what if. As a result, this allows you to positively respond to the situation which will stop the over active fight or flight response.

There have been many people that use mindfulness to control anxiety in their lives who have been able to stop taking medication for the disorder. By learning how to have a different relationship with the feelings they experience, they have continued on to live normal and happy lives.

It has also been found that mindfulness helps those who are suffering from depression because it keeps their mind in the now. Thus not allowing their thoughts to wander back to the past and to all the things that were experienced that caused the depression.

In other words, in order to rid depression and anxiety from our lives, we have to become mindful of the anxiety and depression. Then, as the anxiety and depression reveals itself as a misperception, the symptoms of both will begin to dissipate.

This is not to say that you should stop taking any anxiety or depression medications that have been prescribed for you. If you are taking medication and undergoing therapy at this point you need to continue until your doctor says you no longer need the medication and therapy. Mindfulness is simply meant to get you to that point much faster.

Being mindful will not only help you with anxiety and depression, but it will help you in so many other ways. If you are feeling stressed or overwhelmed, you can use the practice of mindfulness to bring acceptance and peace into your life.

Take me for example, each day I have a ton of projects due. Each day I know if I do not finish what I have said I will complete by that day, I will not get paid. I know if I do not get paid I will not be able to pay my bills and if I cannot pay my bills, my children are going to have to go without and we could lose our home.

That right there can cause a tremendous amount of stress as well as anxiety. By allowing those thoughts to come into my mind, experience it for what it is, reminding myself that of course I am going to complete my work and we are not going to end up homeless, as well as staying mindful while I do my work has allowed me to release a ton of stress from my life.

There was a time when I would wake up before the sun. I would go to bed late into the night and all of the time in between was spent working, trying to make sure all of my projects were finished on time. With a bit of organization as well as practicing mindfulness, I no longer have to go without sleep and work until I am sick to satisfy my anxiety.

I now know I am going to be able to do my projects and everything is going to work out just fine.

## Chapter 11: Instill Compassion In Your Child

Kids who learn compassion will more likely pay attention to their present moment experience. Also, compassion is an attribute that can reduce the impact of his or her own suffering.

How to Instill Mindful Compassion in Your Child

I love the Cheryl Crow lyric: "It's not having what you want. It's wanting what you've got."

Wanting more and better things will never satisfy happiness cravings for long. And, you cannot learn to be compassionate to others unless you are content with what you have. When you are at peace with your life and are satisfied with whatever you are blessed with, you will express gratitude to others and have strong desires to help those less fortunate. Then you can entertain the notion of being happy.

Being at peace means you are able to look around and pay attention to those living with you and around you and seeing it as it is without the blinders on. It is suffering, clear and simple and your child is not desensitized, immune to it or embarrassed by it. With the proper encouragement from you, your children will want to provide those who are suffering with kindness and comfort. I probably won't get too much of an argument that we all desire our kids to live this way.

There are mindful exercises, to instill gracious and thankful behavior in your kids.

List of blessings

Before your kid goes to bed at night, ask him to give you a list of three things that they are grateful for. From my experience, you will hear or read some very endearing and creative items. If you are lucky to have your son or daughter journal at night, it will make for exceptional reading when he or she has kids of their own. Most importantly, it will help your child become aware of the blessings bestowed upon him or her, allowing him or her to express their gratitude fully.

Teach your child the value of helping others

Ask your kids to partake in helping out at your local soup kitchen. If there is no soup kitchen, volunteering at a food bank will do nicely. If your kids are like mine, you will hear anything from a groan to a flat out "no". You might have to be unyielding in this plan. Explain to your kids that you want to participate in helping others to feed your own soul. Do not even suggest it is to make them a better person. Using guilt or suggesting the benefits of this activity will negate the positive impact.

Before you arrive at the soup kitchen, explain to your kids that many people in your community are not as fortunate and need help from time to time. Tell your children that you want to help reduce suffering and are happy to lend a hand.

The impact of this time with your kids is amazing. The benefits are two-fold. First, helping someone in need is heart-warming and secondly, being part of a team that sets up, serves food, cleans dishes or whatever needs being done provides your child a stronger sense of purpose and humility.

Your family bond will strengthen. Your kids will trust you more.

Loving-Kindness Guided Meditation

Guided meditations are when someone leads you during a meditation session to "guide" your mind by their gentle instructions.

They are popular, in part, because it is easier to be mindful when you are being instructed along the way. There is less chance of your mind wandering and getting frustrated or bored with the process.

Of all guided meditations, "loving-kindness" meditations are the most popular. Consider a YouTube search and you will find one for you and your children. They can be 5 minutes or much longer. But the theme is fairly consistent. You will be asked to direct loving-kindness thoughts toward others and accept the loving kindness directed back to you.

My suggestion is to get into the habit of using this technique as a tuck-in at bedtime.

Sending Loving-kindness . . .

I ask them to close their eyes get comfortable. I will hand them a gentle stone to keep them focused on an object. Then I say the following:

Send loving-kindness to yourself
Really love yourself.
Want yourself to be happy.
Think:
I love myself.
May I be free from anger.
May I be free from sadness.

May I be free from pain.
May I be free from difficulties.
May I be free from all suffering.
May I be healthy.
May my body be healthy and strong.
May I be filled with love for others.
May I be happy in my heart
May I be at peace in my heart.
I spread this loving-kindness out: first to my Mom and Dad
May Dad and Mom be free from difficulties.
May they be free from pain and sadness.
May they be free from wanting to collect things
May they be free from all suffering.
May Mom and Dad be healthy and happy.
May they have peace in their hearts
I send loving-kindness to both my brothers and sisters.
May they be free from sadness and anger.
May they be free from all suffering.
May they be happy and free.
May they be free from worrying

May they be well and happy.
May they have peace in their hearts
I send loving-kindness to my teachers and the kids at school.
May they be free from sorrow and suffering.
May they be free from anger and difficulties.
May they be happy.
Free from all difficulties and sadness.
May they be well and happy.
May they have peace in their hearts
I send love now to all the people and all animals and all plants everywhere on this earth.
May all beings on the planet be free from suffering.
May they be free from sadness.
May they be happy, truly happy.
May they be at peace.
I open my heart and accept love and kindness from every being and creature in return.
I let that love into my heart.

May there be peace.

Following the meditation, each child receives a hug/kiss and an "I love you." I lie there for a short time, then leave.

## Chapter 12: Human Being Vs. Human Doing

You are a human being. The human part is the surface self and involves the mind and the body. The being part is the essential self, the part of you this is aware that you exist. Remain connected to the deeper self where you are in touch with your essential awareness, don't get lost in the doing, surface-level stuff.

Shifting perspective

Practice shifting perspective from what is seen (content) to who sees (context). Who is the seer? Who is the knower? Forget about what you see (the content) and focus on who sees (context). Do this with a beautiful, pleasant scene and forget about what you're observing. Focus on who is the observer - who is observing?

Unfulfilled expectations

A fundamental shift required for well-being includes seeing life as it is instead of how we think it should be. For the most part, people experience disappointment and frustration because they have expectations that life should be a certain way. That things should go a certain way, that 'bad things shouldn't happen to me' and they ask 'why is this happening to me?'. Once we begin to live life on life's terms instead of the delusional expectations humans place on life, we actually have a chance to be happy. We give up the expectations like "he should be with me forever", or "I should always be happy".

If you think about something you've ever been upset or unhappy about, it's likely you had an expectation that something or someone should have been a certain way. They weren't and you were disappointed. The only way out of this unhappiness is to identify what your expectation was and to drop it. You stop trying to change them and start taking responsibility for your unhappiness. I'm not unhappy because you got home late, I'm unhappy because I had an expectation that you'd be home in time for dinner. Then you can take empowered action from that stance. If you cling to the complaint that your unhappiness stems from the other person's actions, you remain powerless because they may or may not adjust their behavior in the future. Take responsibility for your part and act accordingly.

Love is the answer for everything.

Love

Love, in it's purest definition means acceptance. It means another sees you as you are and accepts you fully. When you stand in judgment, you are saying that person is not acceptable. You are negating their humanity. Anytime you notice yourself judging, say thank you, because you are being given an opportunity to love. Don't waste time judging yourself because you were judging. Notice the judgment but don't attach any importance to it, don't act from the place of judgment.

Notice what your mind is doing and disregard it.

Once you start being more present, you will notice just how much thinking you do and how much of it involves judgment. It may feel like you're always judging! So yes, your mind is always judging. Within seconds of seeing a person for the first time, you assess their social status, friendliness, etiquette, approachability, sexuality, religion, and how educated they are. You are essentially assessing how useful this person is to you. You use those judgments to determine the person's value. Is this person valuable to me? Can the person help me gain social capital?

Judge the situation or the experience, not the person. Don't diminish their humanity, just note if the situation works for you or not, or if your experience of being with the person energizes you or drains you.

If it works, great, if it doesn't work, no need to name call, criticize or put them down. Just acknowledge that the situation isn't workable for you and move on.

Your brain is hardwired to assess and judge situations in order to assess safety. Humans have the ability to assess emotional safety as well as physical safety. In this regard it is useful and necessary for our survival to employ judgment. Where things go awry is when we begin to judge people. They are this, he is that. She is this way, those people are that way. In this sense, every time we judge people, we limit our ability to connect with them deeply. There is no possibility for a healthy relationship when you have judged a person as being a certain way.

For example, if a person engages in unconscious behavior, you will say he is that way, even if he only did that once. He will always show up for you that way, not because he necessarily IS that way, but because you have put him in a box and won't allow yourself to see him any other way. Having said that, you have the right to choose who is in your life and who is not.

Attachment in Love relationships

Love and attachment are not the same. Attachment in this discussion is not the same as attachment theory. Attachment for the purposes of this conversation refers to a desperate clinging driven by a perceived sense of lack. When you are attached you become reckless because your behavior is driven by selfish motivations. You NEED the other person in order to feel happy and complete. Even if you do 'nice' things for the other person (content), the intention is based on selfishness, which can never be loving and ultimately harms the other person.

When there is attachment you are in a delusional state because your identity believes it's survival depends on the other person. Your madness is covered up until a situation arises that reveals the insanity. He doesn't call, you don't get the promotion. Your madness is exposed. The moment your actions are motivated by attachment they become lifeless. The context is scarcity and desperation. There is no energy or vitality, just a desperate clinging.

Nonattachment in Love

The source of love is always inside you. People come along and bring the experience of love into awareness, and we say we love them. Yes, good, but realize that you are the source of that love, and it can never leave you. They helped you recognize it, experience it, but they can't take it away from you. If you think they are the source of your love, you will cling to them and try to control them in an effort to keep them from ever leaving you. This is addictive attachment. They will feel trapped. True love liberates.

If you really love someone, you will feel that love whether they are next to you, a thousand miles away, and even when they've transitioned. People you love are just there to open your awareness up to that which is already in you. The more you love the more you'll find that you can extend that love to more and more people, until there is only love that emanates from you. You develop a certain reverence for everyone and everything. Who you really are is love, which at it's basic form is just full-acceptance; the absence of judgment.

True love can never leave you. If you love someone, even after the relationship ends (they no longer choose you or through physical death), you will still feel their love.

The reverence for them remains, and you still wish the best for them.

Don't depend on anyone in order to express the love that is you. You be loving of your own volition, not because of somebody else. Don't expect anyone to make you happy. Don't make someone else responsible for making you feel love. See things as they really are. Everything you experience happens within you, not outside of you. You are responsible for the love that you feel. If you want love in a situation, bring love. Be loving. Don't expect anyone else to create that experience for you. It's up to you. This is one of the most liberating shifts that a person can experience.

Love and relationships

Love and relationships are not the same thing. You can love someone and not be in a relationship with them. And you can be in a relationship with someone and not love them. Love is acceptance of the other as they are. This can be very difficult when people live together in a domestic partnership.

To make a loving relationship work, both people have the intention and capacity to offer joy and happiness to one another. The paradox is that you don't expect it from the other, but if the other offers the same to you, it works! The key is to not EXPECT it from the other, but have a mutual understanding that you both intend to offer joy and happiness.

Recognizing that life is painful, you understand that everyone carries some emotional pain. You strive to alleviate and transform their suffering when it emerges. This requires having a deep concern for the other person. You offer reassurance to one another. You say "no matter what, I'm here". "We will get through this."

Engage with the intention to maintain mental calmness and to respond to each other with love especially in difficult situations. This requires seeing the person as your partner, not your enemy. Remain in a state non-attachment.

Remember, if your love has attachment or clinging in it, it is not true love. When you love something, you become one with it. Become one with your partner. Become one with your children. Become one with your family, your friends, your community. Become one with nature. Become one with everything. Love everything. If you have expectations of people, sooner or later they will disappoint you.

A daily exercise to keep you grounded in reality is to remind yourself that you don't need other people for your survival. You switch the context from beggar to one who is whole and complete and is there to offer love instead of needing to get, get, get. Say to yourself silently: I don't need you in order to exist. Then and only then are you truly able to offer unconditional love. A space of freedom moves in and then your interactions will come from a context of true love, not of desperate clinging or addictive need. Focus on what you have to offer instead of what you need to get.

Others can only love you to the capacity that they love themselves. The same is true for you. You can't give what you don't have. You can only love to the capacity that you love yourself.

Reflections on Relationships

If you've had relationships that you don't perceive as positive, ask 'what was this person here to teach me?' Once you learn the lesson, accept the lesson and move on. Some people come into your life to awaken you from some false reality you've created. Their purpose was to help you open your eyes. Then they leave. No relationship lasts forever. Don't lament the amount of time you had with someone and don't stay in something you shouldn't stay in just because you've invested so much time. Accept the impermanence of all relationships.

Anyone who is okay with you being miserable so that they can be happy does not really love you. Your mind might want to go a step further and judge them as 'bad' people. That's not necessary. All that is required is that you see things as they are.

Liking Yourself

If you don't like you, what makes you think other people are going to like you? It's funny how people will dislike themselves so much, but then they expect everybody else to love them. Why would somebody like you if you don't even like yourself?

*Loving Yourself*

Loving yourself is better than hating yourself, but ultimately you want to move away from identifying with thoughts and opinions about how lovable/unlovable you are, because that's just more activity of the mind-made, conceptualized self. If you observe other sentient beings, like dogs, cats, horses, cows, birds, they just are who they are. They are not concerned with loving themselves. They don't have a self-image. They don't have opinions about themselves at all. Let go of having your self-image define who you are. Who you are is the presence behind the thoughts of 'who you think you are'. Just be who you are. Stop needing to define it. Focus on **being** love instead of trying to prove you are lovable.

Stop relating to yourself as somebody who is deprived of love. When you interact with others from the context of deprivation, it robs the both of you of authentic connection.

When you think you need something from someone else, you become a beggar, always trying to get something (appreciation, validation, acknowledgment). And it's never enough. They end up feeling depleted and you end up feeling empty and cheated.

Try to love yourself as much as you want someone else to. Whatever you want from someone else, give it to yourself.

What to do if you can't love yourself

Sometimes you may be so trapped in self-loathing that you feel you couldn't love yourself even if you tried. Sometimes your mind blocks the ability for you to feel the love that is already in you.

If you find you can't love yourself, think of someone you love. This will allow you to immediately access the love that is already inside you.

## Chapter 13: Engaging The Senses

The five senses of touch, smell, sound, taste, and sight are how we learn about the world around us. They help us experience the world and be in the present moment. By practicing the exercises in this chapter, you will learn how to live in the present moment. You will also learn how to isolate the different senses. This helps you identify each of them and can give a better understanding of how emotions interact with the senses.

Touch

Gather several items that feel different, like a ball, marble, stuffed animal, smooth stone, and feather. Have your child close their eyes and hand them each item, one at a time.

"I don't want you to tell me what this is. Don't name it. Tell me what you feel. Is it smooth or rough? Is it hard or soft? Is it round, long, or short?"

As an alternative to this exercise, have your child choose several items while you close your eyes. Ask questions as you did before and try to use what you child describes to identify the item.

*Smell*

Select something fragrant for your child to smell. Perfumes or shampoos work well, but fresh items work better. For example, rose petals, a jasmine flower, mint leaves, a lavender sprig, or a fresh citrus fruit peel. Have your child close their eyes and breathe in the smell, deeply and by waving it slowly in front of their nose.

"How does the smell make you feel? Does it make you feel awake or calm? Does it make your brain feel happy?"

This is an especially useful tool for children who get nervous or anxious. Have them breathe deeply while inhaling the scent. It can work to ground them and calm them.

*Sound*

The sound of a bell ringing is followed by a vibration that moves through the metal. It is a very useful tool for practicing mindfulness. Ring the bell. Instruct your child to put their hand up when they can no longer hear the vibrations from the bell.

"Now, listen to what is happening around you for one minute." Time the child. After one minute, "Describe what you heard. Describe the vibration of the bell and everything you heard in the minute that followed."

Taste

Choose a piece of candy so your child does not know what it is. You can choose something with a simple flavor, like butterscotch or cherry, or something more complex like Pina colada or peaches and cream.

"Breathe in and out while you place this candy in your mouth. Notice how your mouth fills with saliva in response to the taste of the candy. Is the candy sweet? Does it make your mouth pucker? Is it a strong flavor or is it creamy?"

In addition to the simple taste exercise, you can use other foods and ask your child to experience more. Have them close their eyes. Follow a script like the one above, but this time, ask additional questions.

"What does the food feel like? Is it hard or squish? Is it grainy or smooth? What does the food smell like? How does it taste? Would you consider it a good taste or a bad taste?"

Sight

"Pick an ordinary item that you don't normally pay attention to. You can look at the cover of your schoolbook, a bug on a windowsill, or the pattern in the wood of your desk. Look in detail. Notice patterns, indents, marks, and other things that make the item different from everything else. Observe, but do not wonder what happened or why that mark is there. Notice how the pattern or blemish affects the picture or moves with the patterns around it.

Bonus Exercise: Engaging the 'Spidey' Senses

"For this exercise, you are going to engage your inner Spiderman (or Spiderwoman). Lay down or sit with your eyes closed. Think about how you are feeling. Notice the tinglies in your fingertips and the urge to wiggle that you feel in your legs. Do you feel hot or cold? Do you feel awake or tired? What do you hear in this room? Do you see any pictures in your mind? What do you taste? What do you smell? Can you feel anything? Is there any wind moving by you? Do you hear any sounds in the distance?"

This exercise will help your little one describe all the senses as you move through the questions. This teaches them how to notice their body and senses more. Over time, this will give them cues into how they are feeling. This can be especially beneficial for children who are practicing emotional regulation. As they learn to notice certain triggers, they can change their behavior to respond in a more positive way. You should not expect these results immediately, but over time, this simple exercise will grow into something more.

## Chapter 14: The Practice Of Mindfulness Meditation

More often than not, it is alarming for some people to realize how they can be mindless at times as well as how much of their lives they regret or wish away. The good thing is, people can cultivate mindfulness. There are some deliberate mental practices that an individual can apply in order to develop mindfulness just as one can improve his body by conducting physical exercises regularly.

Common Misconceptions

Most mindfulness practices involve some type of meditation. In the West, people usually misunderstand various meditation practices. Thus, it is important to know some of the common misconceptions to avoid them during a mindfulness meditation session.

Not Emptying the Mind

The aim of a mindfulness meditation session is to train the mind to become aware of what it is thinking at all times. Some meditation practices require having a blank mind as well as losing analytical abilities. On the other hand, mindfulness meditation involves being aware of what one is thinking in the present moment. It does not ask one to be dazed or to empty the mind of thoughts.

Not Unmoved by Emotions

More often than not, people hope to be relieved from emotional burdens when they conduct a mindfulness meditation session. This is specifically true when people are in distress. They are inclined to wishing they would be emotionless even for a short period. However, mindfulness meditation has an opposite outcome. Given that mindfulness encourages awareness of the mind's contents, the tendency of an individual is to acknowledge his emotions more vividly and fully. The ability of human beings to notice how they feel heightens once normal defenses are brought down, such as distracting oneself from suffering through eating or entertainment.

Not Retreating from Life

Given that nuns, monks, and hermits refined most meditation practices, many people presume that such practices involve retreating from an interpersonally-rich life. In mindfulness meditation, it is not exactly withdrawing from an interpersonal life although there are several benefits from practicing meditation in a simplified condition. Variations of life are experienced more realistically or intensely during a mindfulness meditation session since one is taking time to being aware of the moment-to-moment occurrence.

Not Searching for Bliss

Most people misunderstand mindfulness meditation as the kind associated with the image of the Buddha smiling blissfully upon them while the rest struggle with empirical reality. In addition, numerous people are inclined to distress when their minds wander, making them feel unsettled or agitated. During mindfulness meditation, pleasant states of mind are allowed to arise and pass; however, the mind does not clinging to the blissful states or reject displeasing ones. The mind simply allows them to flow and pass and then lets go of them.

Not Getting Away from Pain

In mindfulness meditation, an individual increases his capacity to bear pain instead of escaping it. It involves deliberately refraining from automatic actions, which make oneself feel better. For instance, while you are meditating and an itch grows, instead of acting on the urge to scratch, you simply observe the itch and discover any impulses that may arise. This way, you experience actual discomfort or pain in a more vivid way.

Exploring and accepting unpleasant experiences increases one's capacity to bear them. Through mindfulness meditation, one discerns that painful sensations differ from the suffering that goes along with them. In addition, mindfulness meditation allows one to recognize that suffering arises when he reacts to pain with protest, resistance, or avoidance instead of accepting it moment by moment.

Forms of Mindfulness Practice

There are various ways to foster awareness of an occurring experience with acceptance. All of them call for constant practice. Such practice is comparable to improving one's cardiovascular health. An individual might start by carrying out physical exercise daily on his routine, such as riding a bicycle rather than driving to work or taking the stairs rather than using the elevator. Becoming physically fit may also involve setting aside time to carry out exercise formally, such as at a health club or gym. If the individual wants to accelerate the process, he may opt to go on a vacation that is fitness-oriented. This way he can spend most of the day in vigorous exercise. The same is true when it comes to cultivating or fostering mindfulness.

Formal Meditation

This mindfulness practice involves allotting time to regularly go to the "mental gym."

In this practice, an individual regularly sets aside a specific time to sit in meditation in a restful manner. There are numerous types of meditation, which foster mindfulness. Most of them involve picking an object of attention in the initial stage of the practice and returning one's attention to that object every time the mind deviates from focus. The initial stage usually allows an individual to develop a certain level of calmness, which allows him to focus the mind better on the chosen object.

When the mind already established some concentration, mindfulness meditation implicates the mind directly to whatever starts to prevail in the mind. The focus is usually on how the body experiences the event.

The objects of attention may include physical sensations, including an ache, itch, sound, or emotional occurrences manifesting in the body, such as a lump in the throat that develops from sadness or tightness in the chest brought about by anger. Whatever the chosen object of attention is, an individual practices being aware of his present experience and at the same time accepting it.

Daily Mindfulness

This practice involves reminding oneself to pay attention throughout the day to whatever is transpiring in the present moment without changing his routines radically. It entails noticing the experience of, say, the taste of food when one eats; of walking when one walks; and how the surroundings look as one passes through them. Most Zen teachers suggest several techniques for enhancing daily mindfulness. For instance, while driving and the red tail lights of the vehicle in front appear, an individual could try to appreciate their texture as well as color as if he is looking at a magnificent sunset. Another example is when the phone rings, an individual could try to listen to its rhythm and tone as if he is listening to a beautiful musical instrument.

Retreat Practice

This practice involves the "vacation," which is primarily focused on cultivating mindfulness. Just like **daily practice**, there are numerous forms of meditation retreats, which mostly involve extended or long periods of formal practice and often switching from sitting to walking meditation. Meditation retreats are frequently carried out in silence with minimal interpersonal activities with the exception of occasional interviews or conversations with teachers. This entails doing all activities of the day in silence, including getting up, brushing teeth, showering, eating, and doing chores among others. In addition, all these activities are also used as possibilities to practice mindfulness.

It is natural for an individual to feel like being trapped in a room with a madman, specifically for the first few days of a meditation retreat practice. However, it allows one to discover how hard it is be fully committed in the present moment. During a meditation retreat, an individual sees vividly how his minds create suffering. Given that the mind is restless and at times, disturbingly active, it can spin stories about how one is doing and compares oneself to others. There are also times when the mind allows memories of unpleasant emotional events to enter as well as elaborate illusions about the future. On the other hand, most individuals find that the occurrences during an intensive meditation retreat session can transform their lives.

The effects or results of mindfulness practice seem to depend on how often it is carried out. For instance, if an individual carries out a little of daily practice, he also cultivates a little of mindfulness. Therefore, if one does more daily practice as well as adding a regular formal and retreat practices, the effects or outcomes could be more life-transforming.

## Chapter 15: Enjoy Spiritual Awareness

Use your sense of smell
One of the things that can make your senses come to life like nothing else is the aroma of flowers. For this exercise, I want you to visit the florist, rather than just ordering flowers. Take in all of the aromas in the shop and try to buy yourself flowers

that have a great aroma. Talk to the florist. Sometimes you can buy flowers that are renowned for their aroma and that last a long time as well. Lilies are one of these but the white variety is particularly delicate. Take these home and have them in a place where you are greeted by the aroma when you come into your home. Waking up the senses makes you a lot more aware of everything in life and makes you stop and slow down for a moment to appreciate the moment.

Take a walk in the forest or by the beach

The way that we view nature affects how we feel spiritually. After all, whatever God you believe in is responsible for the creation of all the marvelous things around you. We don't take enough time to appreciate nature and our lives are filled to the brim with stress.

Make a point of taking a walk somewhere where there are trees and water, plants and flowers but instead of simply walking through it, take in all of the elements of beauty that are there for you every day of your life, but which you normally take no notice of. It doesn't have to be a long walk. The advantage of a forest is all the oxygen being created by the trees. The advantage of the shoreline is that it always sends such a wave of optimism though you to see the waves lapping up against the shore.

Sit and meditate upon nature

When you meditate upon nature, it's perhaps not as concentrated as meditating in your home but it does a lot for your soul.

Sit in a place that gives you a view of all the wonders of nature and simply lose yourself in being within that moment, seeing all the different elements of nature and understanding how small you are in the order of things. In order to find your spirituality, you have to take yourself back to basics because this gives you the gift of humility. That's a very important gift. Imagine yourself as small as the pebbles on the beach or the leaves on the tree because when you see yourself as that small, you also get to realize that even the smallest of elements in the world holds a place of importance. It makes you more aware of people and of the connection between them and you are able to approach life with a different viewpoint.

Ground yourself

When you do yoga and meditation, you are shown different ways to ground yourself. For instance, if you are doing meditation sitting on a cushion, you sway from one side to another until you feel that the spine is aligned and you are in the best position possible for your meditation session. There are ways to do this in nature too. When was the last time that you put your foot into a babbling brook? How about the last time that you felt the grass beneath your feet or the sand between your toes.

While you are out on your walk take your shoes off for a moment and let your feet feel their footing on the natural surface where you are. This could be on a rock, the earth, the grass, in a stream or anywhere but when you do that for a few moments and then look around you at all the beauty, you feel yourself planted – or at one with nature. Sure, you don't have roots, but the nearer your feet are to the energy of the earth, the more you feel at one with it.

Remember to breathe

Breathing in the air and the ambiance of the places that you go to helps you to fully appreciate them and to be in that moment. As you breathe in and out, let the air go down to your diaphragm, let it sit there for a moment and then breathe out. This is particularly useful after a moment of stress and can be used at any time at all to bring you back into mindful repose. Taste the air, feel the ambiance of your chosen spot and use all of your senses to enjoy the closeness with nature, through sight, sound, ambiance and breath.

## Chapter 16: Step By Step Instructions On How To Perform Meditation: advanced

techniques

Technique One: Fear into Love

Once you find a comfortable position to lie in, preferable crossed legs sitting on a comfy surface. Then what you need to do is take your hands and fold your right hand underneath your left with the palms facing each other. The mysteries behind this is that the left hand is more attached to the heart than the right hand, so that way in a sense you put "love" over everything.

NOTE: This isn't the love you would think of between partners (although it could) but a love for everything, and a love of presenting your gifts to the world. Also that the left hand is connected to the right brain which is dominant in more courageous acts – therefore helping you put yourself out there more for life.

 Then the second part is that once you get into this position is you're going to want to close your eyes and only breathe through your mouth. The reason being is that you want to change the pattern of which your used to doing, cause the brain likes patterns. Breathing through the mouth will create confusion for your mind, and it will begin to submit to new things and ideas. Also breathing through the nose stimulates the brain, this meditation is designed to have your brain create less boggled thoughts in order for you to hear your heart instead.

NOTE: This may get uncomfortable after about ten minutes in, that's why I recommend starting out with a short amount of time first. Also to clarify that this is perfectly safe, and an excellent way in order to try something out of the norm. This meditation is great for those who have a problem taking steps forward and want to jump into things and immerse fully into life without the criticism of others bothering them.

Enjoying the book so far? Leave a review!

Technique Two: No Mind (Gibberish)

Do you tend to chew a lot of gum for some reason, and you don't know why? In my experience after doing this meditation, it helped me release a lot of tension around my neck and jaw especially. The ego is for the most part attached to the face; realize that the ego to a certain degree can also inhibit your bliss in life.

To begin understand this is a cathartic technique, which involves expressive body movements. To start you can either do this in a group or alone – begin with saying nonsense words (gibberish) allow whatever needs to be expressed within just flow out of you. Throw everything out! It doesn't need to make any sense, actually, the less sense the better and just say whatever comes up. Whatever thoughts, sounds, words arise just throw them out. Do this for fifteen minutes.

Then the second part which will also last fifteen minutes is to lie down on your stomach and feel as if you are combing with the earth. As you breathe put extra emphasis on the exhalation as if you were moving one step closer into the earth. This helps recognize the frequencies of which the earth is moving, which in doing so you should take into consideration of moving at this pace in your own life as well.

Technique Three: Kundalini Meditation

The Kundalini Meditation is usually a step down from the Dynamic, and also has one less stage involved in it as well. There are four stages, and each of which will last you fifteen minutes each.

The first stage is to let your whole body vibrate and shake in which way you'd like. Completely be silly, try to imitate a child's pattern of just shaking. As you do this stage you'll see how the energies begin to accumulate from the feet up through the body. Your eyes may be open or closed as well; also lastly remember to not get stuck in one single pattern or movement be animated and change patterns with how you do this considering the brain likes to get fixed with repeating positions.

The second stage is you want to dance, anyway, you feel, or however you'd like. Let your body move as it wishes; side note as for all these stages as well feel free to turn on any music you'd like preferably something more towards instrumental to not really let the words distract you. (Fewer words in the head, more movement and freedom inside the body.)

Third Stage is to close your eyes and to remain standing or sitting in a still position. Just watch what is happening (Imagine yourself turning your eyes inward and witnessing the bodies expression.) Also, take notice of the outer feelings of your body as well.

The last Stage is to just remain still in whatever position you chose while keeping your eyes closed, and just remain still. By being active in the beginning stages you'll recognize how much easier it is by now to ease the thoughts inside your head, and let go of them.

Technique Four: Dynamic Meditation

Before going into this meditation I would like to warn, and state that this is not for beginners necessarily. Please be advised that this is not an ordinary meditation, and should be done with caution. The reason being is that if done properly a significant change will be done within the body after doing this successfully. You'll notice a change within your body and perhaps a slight temporary discomfort in your stomach after doing this. This is normal and natural because it releases the tensions that're held within your body, and is now creating an opportunity for your body to finally in a sense "open up", and not be closed off.

Let's begin: this meditation will have five stages each of them being ten minutes. Feel free though as with any meditation to work your way up to this amount of time. Also, I invite you to try and pick some sort of music that you could have stay repeated throughout this process. You can also do this with people, or alone too.

The first stage is chaotic breathing; it's a form of charging the body. You'll begin by breathing only through your nose violently in and out as fast and chaotic as possible while animating your body. This needs to happen in order to charge the body, and bring the emotions to the surface.

NOTE: In my experience I have done this, and have liked it by I have also tried an exercise called "The Bow" in order to charge the body better, and invite you to look this up as well and try it for yourself.

The second stage will be a catharsis, which is a purging of emotions. Once you have built up a charge inside the body this is the part where you want to let it all out. Express everything you have held inside the body without your head needing to be involved. Whatever emotions come to the surface don't judge them; they could be tears, laughter, anger, yelling, etc.

The third stage is the grounding stage in order for you to make your energy centered. In this stage, you want to remain standing put your hands over your head as high as you can, and jump in the air repeatedly, and land flat footed. With every time you hit the ground you should repeat a deep sounding "Hoo", the word allows breaking up tension in order for energy to reach down into the sex center. Do this until you spend yourself (or ten minutes.)

Fourth stage which I will also invite you to do this stage, and the next for even up to fifteen minutes each (mainly because these aren't exhausting, but more of celebrating.) Immediately after you get done with the third stage you want to just stop freeze, and if you'd like just to lay on the ground. Do not move a muscle, and do not do anything just witness the energies pulsing throughout your body. If a proper state has been reached up until this stage, it's a real enlightening feeling that can't really be explained.

The last stage is rejoicing after the fourth stage feels free to get up and just begin dancing soothingly. Start by swaying your body and let it drift, and dance with the "currents of life". You need not do much here, just remember that you are celebrating at this point.

## Chapter 17: Take Five Minutes

Now that you understand the basics of workplace meditation to control stress, let's examine a specific five minute regimen that will clear your mind and alleviate your stress. This can be performed sitting at your desk. If that is impractical due to the interruptions at your desk, find a quiet place nearby. Some companies have quiet rooms that will enable you to get away from distractions.

The first thing to do is to sit as still as you can with your eyes closed. Try to clear your mind. Then begin to take a series of deep breaths. Slowly inhale through your nose taking a deep breath. Then exhale. Allow the air to flow through your mouth. Repeat this ten times. As you do, you'll begin to feel calmer.

These breaths trigger a relaxation response within the mind. Once you have completed the deep breaths, allow your breathing to return to normal. Now you'll perform a very quick, one minute body scan.

A body scan is the mindful inventorying of the physical sensations in parts of your body. With your eyes closed, begin to focus your attention on your feet. Move progressively to your head. At each body part spend a moment to note any tension you may feel, and then mentally release it. This exercise will bring your mind to rest in the physical present.

After you have scanned your body, you will practice a series of four distinct hand movements associated with Naam Yoga. These techniques, which we discussed a moment ago in Chapter 3, will lessen the stress you feel. In addition, the companion exercises will enable you to feel a greater sense of fearlessness, confidence and intuition.

You will perform each exercise for 15 seconds. The first exercise will be the one we called "Calm." Press your thumb against the indentation between your second and third knuckle on your middle finger. We called the second exercise"Strong". Press your thumb against the side of your index finger between the first and second knuckle.

The third exercise we called"Bold". With index finger and thumb tips from each hand pressed together, push away from your chest as you exhale through your mouth. Draw your hands back as you inhale through your nose. The exercise we called"Savvy"finishes the movement. With your right hand bring your thumb to the tips of your index and middle finger. Then press the finger tips to your forehead above the bridge of your nose. Take the same finger position with your left hand and place it just above your navel.

These exercises will activate sensations of calmness, strength, fearlessness and intuition. With your body in a greater state of relaxation, we can begin to center your mind. Keep your eyes closed and visualize yourself at your desk in a calm state. Now visualize yourself being productive and getting work done. Many experts suggest visualization as merely a means of reducing stress. While this is effective, having performed the earlier exercises in this five minute regimen, your mind should already be calmed.

This visualization technique will enable you to practically apply yourself back to your work. With your stress reduced, your focus should be on stress prevention. Associating the feelings of calm confidence with productivity will help keep stress at bay while you complete the tasks you have at hand.

Some people struggle with visualization. If you are among the many who do, let me clue you in on something that will change your perception of visualization. See,I was a lot like you. I didn't get the whole visualization thing. It seemed to me like it was a bunch of baloney.

Then a friend who was fond of visualization techniques asked me if I remembered something that happened the year before. I told him I did. He asked me to describe the weather of that day. And as I thought back to the high blue skies, the dry air and hot temperatures, he interrupted me.

"You just visualized that day," he told me. I scoffed but then he explained. Memories are a visualization of the past. Visualizations are guiding looks into the future. As I thought about it, I considered the biases with which I recall certain events from my youth and I realized he was right. All this time I was able to visualize, and most of my visualizations were flawed recollections of things past.

Guiding your visualization to the accomplishment of a goal will focus your mind on the surest means to attain your objective. So before you break from your five minute mindful stress relief exercise, take a moment to visualize yourself getting done what you need to do. Then go do it.

So to recap, begin with 10 cleansing deep breaths. Perform a full, but quick, body scan. Then move on to your Naam Yoga hand exercises. And finally, conclude by visualizing your own personal success. In five minutes you will have refreshed, recharged and re-energized yourself.

As I practiced these techniques I found my challenging supervisor to be less troublesome. I was able to cope with the stress he previously evoked. Gradually I didn't feel stress at all. If I was able to do this, you can eliminate the stress you feel from the list you made at the beginning.

## Chapter 18: Mindful Meditation For Family Stress

Family is another major source of stress. Even though you love your spouse and your family the demands of daily life can create a lot of stress that will damage your health and your relationships over time. Running errands like dropping the kids at school, grocery shopping, cooking, cleaning and other household worries can pile up leaving you so stressed out that you don't have the energy to enjoy being with your family.

Mindful Meditation will teach you how to be present and enjoy every moment that you have with your family. Those moments go by so fast that you need to make the most of every moment with your family that you can. But when you have very young children or infants who need constant care and are waking up every few hours all night long it can be a challenge to be present and to be grateful each day.

And when those infants have grown into teenagers they will inspire an entirely different kind of stress as they start to test the limits of your parenting and try out their independence. Mindful Meditation will help you get through it all with as little stress as possible.

The Daily Grind

What causes the most family stress is usually the daily litany of tasks that have to be done in addition to work and other commitments. Driving the kids to school and practices and activities, making sure the shopping gets done, going to the cleaners and making sure the pets are looked after, cooking, doing the laundry, and doing the dishes. All of those tasks can create stress and anxiety for you and your spouse. Taking a few minutes for meditation will help manage that stress.

But how can you fit in time to meditate if you're already running yourself ragged? There are ways that you make time to meditate if you make your own health the priority that it should be.

Make Meditation a Family Activity

Kids can benefit from Mindful Meditation too, so why not make meditating a family activity. Before you sit down to family dinner take a couple of minutes for meditation. Focus not just on your breathing but being present in the moment. Having all of your family gathered together with a good meal to eat and a place to eat in are all things that you should be thankful for. Meditation will help you be present and appreciate the gifts that you have.

Make Meditation a Night Time Activity

As you are getting the kids ready for bed take a few moments for Mindful Meditation. You will be teaching your kids how to manage stress and the importance of being present while you get the benefits of meditation yourself too. Kids who learn how to manage stress early on can avoid some of the health problems associated with stress later on. And Mindful Meditation can help kids learn to focus and avoid developing school related anxiety like test anxiety.

Making Time for Yourself

When you are juggling work and a relationship and family obligations it can seem like there's never any time for yourself. But you have to make your own self-care a priority and that includes making time for mindfulness.

Carving out a few minutes for yourself each day can change the quality of your life forever. You will be healthier, happier, less anxious and less stressed out all the time. Your relationships with everyone around you, including yourself, will improve.

If you have a schedule that is packed with responsibilities you may need to get creative about finding time to meditate.

This list of ways to fit some meditation time into your day is filled with tips from real people who have found clever ways to take care of everyone else and take care of themselves too:

Get up 30 minutes early. You might hate losing the sleep, but the benefits of meditation will make up for the sleep.

Turn off the TV an hour earlier at night. Are you really watching that show or just listening to it in the background? Turn it off and go meditate.

Turn off your tablet, computer and smartphone. If you are checking emails and surfing the Web before bed you have to time to meditate. Facebook can wait, but your self-care can't. Turn it off and go meditate.

Make lunches the night before. The 20 minutes you spend making lunches in the morning could be time to mediate. Make all the lunches the night before and have them ready to go in the morning.

Make breakfast in the slow cooker. There will be a hot meal waiting when you get up and you will have 15 minutes that you can use to meditate. Slow cooked oats in the slow cooker are delicious and healthy.

Make meals ahead of time. Once a week cook up some casseroles or other dinners. Freeze them so that you can just pull out a healthy dinner during the week when you are busy. You can use the time while it's cooking to meditate.

Take more baths. Baths are a great place to meditate because it's quiet time when no one else will bother you. Or, if you don't have time for a bath meditate in the shower. Stand under the hot water and be present. It will refresh your mind and your body.

Leave for work 10 minutes earlier. You can sneak in a quick meditation in your car before you go into the office. It's a good way to start the day focused and ready to work.

Skip practices. You don't need to watch every sports practice or activity that your child does. While your child is busy head back to the car to get a little Mindful Meditation time. It will help you release all the stress of the day so that you can focus on your family at night.

Go for a walk. Meditation doesn't have to be done sitting down and being perfectly still. Leave the MP3 player at home and go for a walk in your neighborhood, even if it's just around the block. Breathe in the fresh air and notice the beautiful world around you.

Mindfulness for Tough Situations

Mindfulness, especially Mindful Meditation, can add a lot to your quality of life when you practice it regularly. It's a great tool to help manage stress and anxiety in your daily life. But mindfulness is also a powerful tool to have in tough or emergency situations. When you have panic attacks, or anxiety attacks, or when you are battling the symptoms of Depression and feel like you are losing ground. When you feel like you are totally alone and losing the battle mindfulness can help you fight back and find your center once more.

Mindfulness and Anxiety Attacks

Anxiety attacks can come out of nowhere and they can be so intense that you feel like you're having a heart attack. When they are really bad you might feel like the room is spinning or like you can't catch your breath. It's in that moment that mindfulness can help you.

When you feel your heart start to race and you feel your breath getting shallow stop right where you are. Close your eyes. Focus only on your breath. Feel the breath flowing in and out of your body. Let your thoughts race, just try to bring them back to your breath every few breaths.

Just think about breathing. Your breath will start to get deeper. Your heart will stop racing. Your adrenal glands will stop pumping adrenaline and cortisol through your body. You will relax, and then you can deal with whatever caused the panic attack.

If you have an anxiety disorder sometimes panic doesn't hit as an attack, it comes in waves, washing you over you when you need to do everyday things like go to the grocery store, or pick up medication at the pharmacy. Mindfulness can help you stop the waves of anxiety.

When you focus on being present just in the moment you aren't thinking about when the next wave of anxiety will hit or worrying about how many more waves are coming. You can break the anxiety cycle by being present in the moment and staying present in the moment.

Mindfulness Tools for Panic and Anxiety

When you're in a panic state it is sometimes difficult to be mindful. Using a guided meditation smartphone app or listening to a meditation can help you focus when you are so panicked that you can't focus. You can also write out a mantra or repeat a mantra to yourself to help you focus.

If going out is a trigger for your anxiety, keep a small card in your wallet with a mindfulness mantra on it that you can pull out and look at if you need to. Or, keep a notepad and pen in your bag or in your car so that you can write out the mantra over and over to help yourself focus. A simple but effective mantra like "Breathe in peace. Breathe out stress. I am safe" is really all you need.

You may even want to record yourself repeating a mantra, or reciting a guided meditation that you can listen to. The sound of your own voice might be soothing when you are panicked.

You also can arrange a signal with a friend to let them know that you are panicking and need a mindfulness reminder. An example of this type of arrangement might be texting a code word like "tree" to your friend who would receive the text and know by the use of the code word that you were panicking. The friend could then call or text you to help you focus and calm down.

Mindfulness and Depression

According to a recent study (Lu, 2015) mindfulness is proving to be one of the few treatments that is effective for treating Depression relapses and symptom reoccurrences. The study that was done found that mindfulness was a very effective way for people diagnosed with Depression to manage their symptoms when the symptoms that had previously been treated came back.

Mindfulness is an effective treatment for Depression because it breaks the cycle of negative thoughts and emotions as well as the focus on the past and the future. People with Depression can suffer from anxiety about actions in the past or what might happen in the future. By teaching them to focus their thoughts only on the present moment they can stop that negative cycle and stop the symptoms of Depression from becoming so intense that they impact the quality of life.

Mindfulness is an easy way for anyone to fight Depression, no matter what their age, experience or level of Depression. Instead of having to spend months finding the right drug to treat their individual Depression they can practice Mindful Meditation and get almost immediate relief from the symptoms that are making their lives difficult.

Since mindfulness has no side effects and is 100% safe and effective it can make a huge impact in the lives of people who have chronic Depression that doesn't respond to other treatments. Mindfulness is giving new hope to people who have struggled with Depression all their lives.

## Chapter 19: Why You Should Visualize

So far we've looked at using meditation and cognitive restructuring to change our mental states. But actually, it might be the case that visualization is even more useful and even more important.

Most people believe that we think in 'thoughts'. That is to say that we have an inner monologue that works like the thought boxes in comic books. More recent research though suggests that we can think in lots of modalities: sometimes we visualize, sometimes we imagine our bodies doing something and almost 'feel' what we're thinking and sometimes we just 'know'. This latter example is called 'unsymbolized thought'.

And in fact, thinking with our bodies and our senses might just be what enabled us to develop thought in the first place…

Embodied Cognition

Briefly, embodied cognition is the idea that all our thoughts eventually relate back to physical experience.

When someone says something to you, or when you think something, your brain interprets this in such a way that gives it meaning. You don't inherently understand language, which means the brain must be 'translating' it into some kind of pure meaning.

Psychologists once believed that the brain had a language of its own that they called 'mentalese'. More recently though, more and more experts adopted the belief that we understand things by visualizing them. When someone says tells you a story, you understand the story because your brain visualizes it happening to you.

When someone tells you they walked through the snow, you visualize the color white, you imagine the cool air on your skin and you almost hear the sound of the crunching snow underfoot. When we think 'higher level' thoughts, we understand them only because we can relate them back to physical experiences via abstraction. Maths after all is fundamentally based on counting…

This is also consistent with the idea that areas of our brain light up during visualization just as though we were really engaging in the action. If you imagine swinging a golf club, then neurons relating to that movement will fire in your brain.

And as far as your brain and body is concerned, that might as well be happening!

So it makes a lot of sense to combine visualization with your meditation training and with your restructuring. Don't believe that visualization can 'trick' your brain into thinking something is happening and thereby alter your emotional state? Then just try relieving your most upsetting moments, or imagining scenes from a very sad movie. You'll start to feel incredibly sad in no time…

Visualization for Productivity

One way to use this power of visualization that is well understood, is to go to a 'happy place' during meditation. If you can't meditate in a calm and beautiful environment, then at least you can simulate it in your mind's eye by imagining you're on a beautiful beach, in a log cabin in the mountains, or in a large field getting plenty of sun.

But you can also use visualization in order to alter your emotional state in other ways.

For example, if you're struggling to focus on your work, then you might utilize visualization to create a little eustress to motivate you. To do this, you simply need to remember **why** you're doing the work and why it's important to you. Let's say that you're working towards a presentation for a meeting: visualize just how great it would feel to conquer that presentation and knock it out the part. Then visualize what doing that repeatedly could one day lead to: a better career and a better salary for instance.

Now visualize the opposite: imagine it going wrong and remember why it matters.

You can do the same thing with almost anything you're struggling to focus on. By linking what you're doing back to the emotional hook and the reason you're doing it, you can much more effectively find the determination and drive you need to complete it. Keep your goals in mind and you'll be much more motivated every day to get out of bed and start working out, or to work on your personal project, or to put in your very best performance at work.

## Conclusion

Thanks for grabbing this book. I hope you've gained insight into what it takes to live a mindful life.

Over the years, I've noticed the impact being mindful has had on my daily life. The change has been a positive one. It took time to get used to all the changes I was making but the results were well worth the initial struggle. The relationships in my life have all improved and I found I could live my life aware and in the moment.

Don't be afraid to transform your life into the one you desire. This book gives you all the tools you'll need to get started. Check the resources section if you have any further questions that weren't answered.

Good luck! I wish you all the best!